KIERKEGAARD

History and Eternal Happiness

Vivaldi Jean-Marie

University Press of America,® Inc.
Lanham · Boulder · New York · Toronto · Plymouth, UK

Copyright © 2008 by
University Press of America,® Inc.
4501 Forbes Boulevard
Suite 200
Lanham, Maryland 20706
UPA Acquisitions Department (301) 459-3366

Estover Road
Plymouth PL6 7PY
United Kingdom

All rights reserved
Printed in the United States of America
British Library Cataloging in Publication Information Available

Library of Congress Control Number: 2008930726
ISBN-13: 978-0-7618-4145-6 (paperback : alk. paper)

⊖™ The paper used in this publication meets the minimum
requirements of American National Standard for Information
Sciences—Permanence of Paper for Printed Library Materials,
ANSI Z39.48—1984

Pour Devi qui porte la vérité sur son joli visage

Contents

Preface	vii
Introduction	1
Kierkegaard's Critique of Romanticism and German Idealism	5
Climacus's *Philosophical Fragments*	17
Climacus's *Concluding Unscientific Postscript*	85
Notes	121
Index	131

Preface

Kierkegaard's *Philosophical Fragments* and *Concluding Unscientific Postscript* are two important texts in Kierkegaardian literature. Kierkegaard's ongoing reflections on Christianity and Philosophy find their most vehement expression in these two books. They bear the elaboration Kierkegaard's adage that genuine Christian experience is inseparable from subjective appropriation against Modern Philosophy as the main challenge that threatened the possibility of such experience. In these two texts, the pseudonym author, Johannes Climacus, is striving voraciously to do justice to both, Modern Philosophy and Christianity. In the spirit of the nineteenth century and the ascendancy of Hegelian thought in Europe, Climacus is responding to the menace that the potency of Hegel's Philosophy poses to Christianity. The imminent threat that Christianity is facing in the nineteenth century is the dissolution of God and the authentic Christian experience within History. It is in attempting to circumvent such threat that *Philosophical Fragments* and *Concluding Unscientific Postscript* are classic religious and philosophical texts of their period.

Johannes Climacus wishes to limit both, Philosophy and Christianity while attempting simultaneously to preserve their authentic aspects. The beauty of Climacus's investigation consists in that it is free of fanaticism; Climacus is critical of Modern philosophers while capturing the aspects of their thought that are favorable to the possibility of subjective and authentic Christian experience. By the same token, Climacus refuses to swallow whole the prevailing Christian approaches of his native Copenhagen and the nineteenth century. Climacus is critical of the scientific attitudes of the theologians of his time toward Christianity. The need to critically assess both, Modern Philosophy and Christianity leads to the relentless reflection upon History and the enumeration of its shortcomings. For Climacus, the embodiment of the historical attitude, as the earthly approach to subjective experience, is Socrates who stands as the highest Hellenic individuality. Socrates's defiance and sincere engagement with each learner is the prototype in the finite context of the Hellenic. The positive outcome of Socrates's finitude is that it accentuates the need for another higher form of experience. Socrates is a mere midwife; he witnesses and participates in birth giving, but cannot give birth himself. Climacus introduces Jesus Christ—*the savior and condition*—as the completion of Socrates's project and the infinite Messiah who is empowered to witness birth and give birth to followers. Whereas Socrates was only a witness, Jesus Christ is both, the progenitor of his apostles and their witness in faith. Thus, under the light of Climacus's ambition in the *Philosophical Fragments* and *Concluding Unscientific Postscript*, we are reading the conversation between Socrates and Jesus Christ as well as between Hegel and Kant, Kant and Fichte. Then, Climacus brings the outcome of each philosophical conversation to bear upon the subjective and religious conversation between Socrates and Jesus Christ. Metaphorically, these two texts are comparable to a large room in which Climacus serves as the mediator of a dialogue between Socrates, Jesus Christ, Kant, Fichte, Hegel, the Romantics, and Lessing. Accordingly, the following project proceeds to remain as loyal as possible to what is said in the room. It is written in the spirit of fair journalism and philosophical exegesis while being congenial to novice of Kierkegaardian literature and scholars. Throughout the composition, the guiding thought has been to write a piece that Climacus and Kierkegaard would have deemed to be fair to the religious and philosophical objectives of the *Philosophical Fragments* and *Concluding Unscientific Postscript*.

Faithful elaboration of the exchange that takes place between the members of each tradition is meant to cast Kierkegaardian literature under a different perspective. It is intended to contribute to free Kierkegaard's corpus from the shackles of Existentialism and Subjectivism. Kierkegaard's engagement with Modern Philosophy and Christianity is the proof that his philosophical project is rooted solidly in the post-Kantian tradition of the nineteenth century and that it is philosophically inaccurate to consider Kierkegaard's corpus without the Christian issues that drive his intellectual production. Hopefully, the project contributes to strengthen Kierkegaard's corpus as a series of reflections upon Christianity and Philosophy.

The thesis that emerges in the conclusion of the project unfolds from the exegesis of the *Philosophical Fragments* and *Concluding Unscientific Postscript*. Mainly that the notions of *Religiousness A* and *Religiousness B* that Climacus introduces at the conclusion of the *Concluding Unscientific Postscript* maps out the possibility of authentic religious experience by allowing the self's subjectivity to be aware of its intensity and readiness prior to committing to any religious creed. Religious experience can only be deeper given that the self's subjectivity chooses to be religious in freedom. In agreement with Kierkegaard's wish to write for individual readers, the project is formulated in lucid language in order to avoid confusion about the texts and to invite individual reflection on the objective of Johannes Climacus.

Vivaldi Jean-Marie
03/18/08 Brooklyn, NY

Introduction

At first, writing about the *Philosophical Fragments* may seem a paradoxical endeavor. The seeming paradox consists in the fact that the nature of the text, which Johannes Climacus states in the *Preface*, is meant to be a humble and fragmented thought experiment. The purview of the text is not definite; Climacus emphasizes that it is not systematic. It is not a final account of the solution to one specific or a set of philosophical problems. On the other hand, writing about a text presupposes that there is a specific thesis to derive from it. Acknowledging this fact compels the present attempt to write about the text to be loyal to Climacus's goal and to try to reveal the underlying themes and incentives of his *Philosophical Fragments*.

Despite Climacus's wish, *Philosophical Fragments* is a philosophical masterpiece in virtue of its bluntness and the rigorous investigation of philosophical and Christian issues. It is immanent because it sets out to carry out such investigation without any sets of assumptions or any intended solution; the account is not teleological. Climacus seems to be suggesting that the project is carried out *ex nihilo*. Climacus asserts that he does not have answers, but questions. Thus the exposition opens up with the following questions: "*Can a historical point of departure be given for an eternal consciousness; how can such a point of departure be of more than historical interest; can an eternal happiness be built on historical knowledge?*" These questions prelude the two dominant themes of the text, mainly, the historical and eternal. *Philosophical Fragments* unfolds upon the dynamic of the historical which provides the occasion for the rise of eternal consciousness.

It is noteworthy that Climacus could have phrased it differently as: "*The way that a historical point of departure can be the basis of eternal consciousness; the way that such a point of departure can be more than mere historical interest; how an eternal happiness is built on historical knowledge.*" Such prelude would be standard for a philosophical exposition which starts out to prove a specific thesis. Instead, Climacus is hoping for answers to the above queries; in earnest and humility, Climacus wants to allow the answers to come forth on their own. Such approach renders the project autonomous. It is thus that Climacus's project is immanent; the conclusion is to come forth from within the questions themselves.

Hence, as a commentary on *Philosophical Fragments* and its companion piece, *Concluding Unscientific Postscript*, the project strives to remain loyal to Climacus's vision by attending to the questions that drive these two texts and the philosophical tradition with which they are conversing. The unifying thread that the present project hopes to show is Johannes Climacus's heritage from Modern Philosophy and his critique of their account of History, religious experience, and subjectivity. The analysis of Climacus's critical approach toward Modern Philosophy is going to yield that his goal is to point out the possibility of a Modern religious experience. In the conclusion, on the basis of Climacus's investigation in the two texts it will be shown that Climacus is leaning toward a Modern view of subjectivity and religious experience.

The central notion that animates the exposition is the *moment* which is the natural outcome of Climacus's view of the ideal teacher personified in Socrates and the Platonic account of knowledge as recollection. For Climacus, the teacher is an occasion; she is a medium through which the learner reconnects with latent inner knowledge. Hence in prioritizing and focusing on the person of the teacher, the learner runs the risk of being misled and to view the teacher as the source of knowledge, instead of the occasion to awaken inner knowledge. Knowledge dwells within the learner already. The aspect of the epistemological exchange that Climacus believes to be pivotal is the moment. The moment represents the aspect that is unprecedented; it is *a priori*. The moment is the ground that makes the epistemological act feasible. It is in virtue of its *a priori* status that Climacus grants it *atemporal* status.

Climacus's account suggests that he holds subjective truth as the essence of the self. It is that which grants authenticity to the self. For Climacus, the self becomes authentic by recollecting the truth with the assistance of the teacher and the innate condition. As long as one has not undergone the process, "He is, then, untruth." The initial role of the teacher is to bring the learner to acknowledge that she is essentially untruth. The first phase of the epistemological act is to make the learner know that she doesn't know. This requirement is reminiscent of the Christian act of redemption, which cleanses the soul. This fact is manifest in Socrates whose motto is ignorance; the recognition that he does not know anything. For Climacus, the teacher is one who sets the learner free from illusions; the teacher exposes the learner to her untruth. Freeing the learner from untruth is the preliminary aspect of coming to subjective truth. Hence, Climacus regards and uses Socratic teaching as redemptive; it carries out the spiritual purification prior to upbuilding.

Climacus insists that the condition to enter truth is intrinsic to the learner. It is an essential constituent that the learner receives in being created. The role of the teacher would be futile if the condition were not intrinsic to the learner. Under Climacus's analysis, ignorance represents the deliberate denial of subjective truth; ignorance is repressed subjective truth. Untruth is willful ignorance and thus sin; the offence is rooted in subjectivity. By asserting that sin is willful ignorance and untruth, Climacus is alluding to the Fall and the deliberate decision of Adam and Eve to become sinful. Sin, as the outcome of the Fall, is the willful repression of the innate condition to be in truth. For Climacus, the learner must willfully unveil the condition that is latent in the self to overcome untruth. Returning to the condition is imperative in order to overcome the sinful state that all the descendants of Adam inherited from the Fall. The process is complete in the leap or the act of faith which transcends the historical to embrace the eternal nature of Jesus Christ.

For Climacus, deliverance from sin and untruth may start with Socrates, as an earthly teacher and *rédempteur*. However, the transformation that the learner must undergo requires divine intervention. It is at this juncture that it becomes evident that Climacus begins with Socrates and then presupposes Jesus Christ, as the Christian savior, to complete the process although he does not overtly name Jesus Christ. Both, Socrates and Jesus Christ aim at awakening the learner and disciple to subjective truth. The requirement for the transformation of the learner is beyond the terrestrial qualification of Socrates. Climacus starts with Socrates because the essence of the Socratic approach is that once the learner has appropriated the truth, she can transcend Socrates, as the teacher. The nature of the Socratic approach makes the transition to the divine feasible. In introducing the notions of the god and savior, Climacus has gone beyond Socrates and is implicitly discussing the mission of Jesus Christ as the Messiah. Socrates is the *rédempteur* who precedes Christ in preparing the learner to accept the gospel, the good news, as the apex of the Christian experience.

The moment is thus both, historical and eternal because it occasions the transition from temporality and defines the eternal vocation of the self. For Climacus, the singular moment stands as the fullness of time. It is through the fullness of time that the learner is reborn. The moment is a hybrid of the historical and eternal aspects of the project that Climacus aims at reconciling. The temporal aspect of the moment constitutes the historical that Climacus wants to merge with the mission of Christ. The medium that Climacus is using to link the historical with the experience of eternal happiness is Philosophy. His account of the savior and the god, as teacher, presents a philosophical account of the manifestation of Jesus Christ, which is preceded by the earthly Socrates. The crux of the project is to attempt to bring together the manifestation of Jesus Christ within the domain of faith and understanding which operates according to reason. Climacus's aim is to unite two different fragments of the self. In the *Fragments* and *Concluding Unscientific Postscript*, Climacus is bridging the two polar figures, who permeate Kierkegaard's corpus, mainly, Socrates as the *rédempteur* and the Hellenic embodiment of the understanding with Christ as the savior and apex of the Christian experience.

Kierkegaard's Critique of Romanticism and German Idealism

Romantic Irony

Before turning to the exposition of the *Philosophical Fragments* and *Concluding Unscientific Postscript*, it is necessary to draw out the main aspects of Modern Philosophy that Johannes Climacus relies on in the attempt to address the issue of the relationship of historical knowledge and eternal happiness. The goal of this section is to bring forward the Romantic and Idealist notions that are pervasive in the exposition of the *Fragments* and *Postscript*. It is noteworthy that Climacus considers German Idealism and Romanticism as the completion of Modern Philosophy. The explanation of these notions will make it easier to depict their implicit use in the texts. One of the dominant Romantic ideas that are present in Climacus's texts is Irony. Kierkegaard develops the concept of Romantic Irony early in his intellectual formation. His dissertation—*The Concept of Irony* (1841)—provides an analysis of Socratic Irony and Modern Irony. In this text, Kierkegaard elaborates the essential aspects of Socratic Irony, and devotes the section—*Irony after Fichte*—to elucidate the origin of Romantic Irony in Fichte's Philosophy while assessing its application by Romantics such as, Schlegel and Tieck. This section of Kierkegaard's dissertation is important because it is the explicit basis of the concept of Irony that is ubiquitous in the pseudonymous authorship. Also, the account of Irony in *The Concept of Irony* will be relevant to the infrastructure of the *Fragments* and *Postscript* that is to follow and the pseudonymous nature of Johannes Climacus.

The section—*Irony after Fichte*—bears the expression of Kierkegaard's views of the German Idealists: Kant, Fichte, Hegel, and their influence upon Romantic figures such as Schlegel, Tieck, and Solger. The views that Kierkegaard presents in this piece recurs in the corpus under implicit form. Kierkegaard begins with a bold assertion of the shortcoming of Kant's Philosophy. According to Kierkegaard's critical lens, positing the *in-itself* as being impervious to thought represents the failure of Kant's Philosophy because it alienates thinking from what is closest to it, mainly the self. Kierkegaard expresses his position on Kant's Philosophy metaphorically in the following: "Philosophy walked around like a man who is wearing his glasses and nevertheless is looking for his glasses—that is, he is looking for something right in front of his nose and therefore never finds it...this externality, this *Ding an sich*, constituted the weakness in Kant's system. Indeed, it became a question whether the *I* itself is not a *Ding an sich*."[1] The problem with Kant's account of the *in-itself* is that it leaves the *I* bereft of any finite content. It posits the *in-itself* as an infinite entity that is beyond the limited grasp of the *I*. For Kierkegaard, it is problematic because it impoverishes the self in reducing it to a mere epistemological duality. Kant's position is the preliminary move through which German Idealism proceeds to reduce the Modern self to a mere particular, which is oppressed by the tyranny of the universal.

Kierkegaard then praises Fichte for recognizing and overcoming the limit and inherent challenge of Kant's Philosophy that result from the dichotomy of the self and the *in-itself*. In Kantianism, the self is left to revolve within its impoverished sphere without being hypostatized by what is closest to it. Fichte's achievement is to have demonstrated that the *in-itself* belongs within the self. Kierkegaard believes that Fichte's accomplishment infinitizes the *I* or the self. In Fichte's Philosophy, the *I* is both, the spontaneous author of its creations and the creations themselves; the self stands as absolute. "This question was raised and answered by Fichte. He removed the difficulty with this *an sich* by placing it within thought; he infinitized the *I* in *I-I*. The producing *I* is the same as the produced *I*. *I-I* is the abstract identity. By so doing he infinitely liberated thought."[2] However, the infinite freedom of thought comes with a price. Fichte's infinitizing of the *I* remains fruitless because the *I* never absorbs any fixed and determinate content. For Fichte, Kierkegaard thinks, the infinite nature of the *I* consists in its unending striving, which leaves its constitution continually sterile. The bare self is enmeshed in the perennial anxiety of seeking content.

> But this infinity of thought in Fichte is, like all Fichte's infinity (his ethical infinity is ceaselessly striving for the sake of this striving itself; his esthetic infinity is ceaselessly producing for the sake of this producing itself; God's infinity is ceaseless development for the sake of the development itself), negative infinity, an infinity without any content. When Fichte infinitized the *I* in this way, he advanced an Idealism beside which any actuality turned pale, an acosmism in which his Idealism became his actuality even though it was Docetism. In Fichte, thought was infinitized, subjectivity became the infinite, absolute negativity, the infinite tension and urge.[3]

For Kierkegaard, Fichte's Philosophy lacks any finite telos given that the infinity to which it aspires is being negated in the process. It is on the basis of this claim that Kierkegaard regards the Fichtean account of infinity to be merely negative; it never settles upon positive reality as transcendent. The self enjoys total flexibility in Fichte's Philosophy. Thus, the shortcoming of Fichte's Philosophy is the opposite of that of Kant's, because it infinitizes the self and renders it incommensurable to reality, whereas Kant infinitizes the *in-itself* and sets it beyond the grasp of the self. Kierkegaard reaches the conclusion that: "Kant lacks the negative infinity, Fichte the positive."[4]

It is in virtue of its complete flexibility that the Fichtean self stands as the absolute determining factor that structures its world according to its infinite position. "The I became the constituting entity."[5] However, given the negativity of its infinite nature, the *I* remains as infinite potential in relation to which the finite domain is inadequate. The negative infinity of the *I* makes it alien to finitude. Kierkegaard characterizes the Fichtean *I* in the following: "It is a potentiation, an exaltation as strong as a god who can lift the whole world and yet has nothing to lift."[6] Kierkegaard thinks that Fichte merely succeeds in reversing the problematic relation of thought and the *in-itself* in Kant's Philosophy.

The discussion of Kant's and Fichte's philosophies is propaedeutic to Kierkegaard's accounts of Romantic Irony. Kierkegaard contrasts Kant's and Fichte's accounts of the *I* in order to focus on the contribution of the latter to Schlegel's and Tieck's concepts of Romantic Irony. Also, the analysis of Kant's and Fichte's accounts present Kierkegaard's reception of his contemporaries in the philosophical circle of Copenhagen. Kierkegaard, like many of his contemporaries, believes that Fichte's infinitizing of the *I* is at the basis of Romantic Irony. Schlegel and Tieck were insightful in discovering the meritorious aspect of the Fichtean *I*, which is its constituting power. "This Fichtean principle that subjectivity, the *I*, has constitutive validity, is the sole omnipotence, was grasped by Schlegel and Tieck, and on that basis they operated in the world."⁷ It is on the ground of the constitutive power of the *I* that Schlegel and Tieck develop their views of the relationship between the self and its surrounding. The distinctive mark of the Irony that results from Schlegel's and Tieck's appropriation of the constitutive power of the *I* is its thorough negation of historical actuality in order to generate a world that reflects strictly the inner experience of the *I*. For Kierkegaard, the core of Romanticism consists in its development of the ironic ability of subjectivity; Romanticism and Irony are interchangeable for Kierkegaard. "Throughout this whole discussion I use the terms 'Irony' and 'ironist'; I could just as well say 'Romanticism' and 'Romanticist'. Both, terms say essentially the same thing;"⁸

Schlegel's and Tieck's notions of Irony apotheosize subjectivity by granting it total control in determining its world. "Here we perceive that this Irony was not in service of the world spirit. It was not an element of the given actuality that must be negated and superseded by a new element, but it was all of historical actuality that it negated in order to make room for a self-created actuality."⁹ Besides, Kierkegaard thinks that it is due to its complete detachment from historical reality that Hegel was opposed to Romantic Irony. The possibility of subjective Irony is twofold; it can choose to deny reality or may determine it according to the self's subjective disposition. In its infinite standpoint, the negativity of the ironic subjectivity cancels historical actuality, as well as asserts it. "Irony now functioned as that for which nothing was established, as that which was finished with everything, and also as that which had the absolute power to do everything. If it allowed something to remain established, it knew that it had the power to destroy it, knew it at the very same moment it let it continue."¹⁰ The Romantic position toward actuality is further illuminated by their refutation of any absolute ground. As Frank observes: "The skepticism of the early German Romantics is targeted precisely against a program of absolute foundations. They question whether there is immediate knowledge and find Jacobi's appeal to faith an untenable solution to the problem of the unknowability of the absolute. According to the Romantic position, our knowledge is situated in an infinite progression and has no firm, absolute foundation."¹¹ The rejection of absolute foundations has far reaching impact in the relationship of the self and its social context.

Furthermore, the freedom of ironic subjectivity has an impact on ethics and morality as well. Kierkegaard believes that the negation of reality that the subjective ironist carries out threatens the existence of ethics and morality since they represent the bases of reality. The ironist deems herself to be above morality and ethics on the presupposition that reality may not have any foundation beside the determinations of subjectivity. "The ironist stands proudly inclosed within itself, and just Adam had the animals pass by, he lets people pass before him and finds no fellowship for himself. In so doing, he continually collides with the actuality to which he belongs. Therefore it becomes important for him to suspend what is constitutive in actuality, that which orders and supports it: that is morality and ethics. "[12] Even though Kierkegaard is here critical of the ironist's attitude toward ethics and morality, the ironist's ability to suspend the ethical is later assumed in the account of Abraham's transcendence of the ethical in *Fear and Trembling*, and within the inward disposition of *Religiousness A* in the *Postscript*. The exception consists in the fact that Kierkegaard posits the ethical stage as a necessary phase in the evolution of the self, which is personified in the corpus as *Judge William*. On the other hand, the Romantics remain indifferent toward Ethics.

As it will be developed in the last section of the project, which focuses on the *Postscript*, the world-historical in contrast to the humorist and religious individual is the one who regards historical actuality as absolute from an ethical perspective. Unlike the humorist and religious, the world-historical individuality is absolutely bound to the ethical norms that govern its historical situation. In his characterization of the humorist and religious, Climacus presupposes the ability of subjective Irony to distance itself from historical finitude. The account that Kierkegaard provides in the dissertation is illustrated in the attitude of the humorist toward historical actuality; Irony is thus the incognito cloak of both, the humorist and religious when dealing with social reality. The humorist may contemplate the events of historical actuality as comical in virtue of subjective Irony. The attitude of *Religiousness A*, which makes it possible to deepen subjectivity independently of all transcendence, presupposes subjective Irony. This will be further elaborated in the final section.

In addition, the Fichtean heritage of Romantic Irony is implicit within the pseudonymous nature of Johannes Climacus himself. Climacus illustrates the ironist attitude through his detached relation toward the exposition of the *Fragments* and *Postscript*. As Climacus asserts in the *Preface* of the *Fragments*, he is only putting thought at the service of the issue. It is by the means of his ironic stance that Climacus claims that he can only 'stake his life in the exposition since it is all that he has to offer'. The underlying Irony of Climacus culminates in the declaration in the conclusion of the *Postscript* that he is a humorist. The inward deepening of the humorist, that Climacus asserts himself to be, is feasible upon the basis of an ironic disposition.

Kant's In-Itself

The role of the *in-itself* in Kant's thought is one of the dominant aspects that run throughout Kierkegaard's intellectual production. Kierkegaard regards Kant's philosophical achievement as a central stage in the development of absolute Idealism. "One affinity between Kant and Kierkegaard is that the latter embraces implicitly the notion that human cognition has the inherent tendency to extend itself beyond its allowable limits."[13] Also, the critical approach of Kant's transcendental system is conducive to the attempt of Idealism to show how thought evolves toward grasping the infinite. For Kierkegaard, this ambition of Idealism represents the core of Modern Philosophy, which begins with Kantianism. In a journal entry, Kierkegaard records the following claim: "On the whole, one has to say that Modern Philosophy, even in its most grandiose forms, nevertheless is really only an introduction to making it possible to philosophize. Hegel undeniably completes—but only the development that had its beginning with Kant and was directed toward knowledge."[14] Modern Philosophy begins with Kant and ends in Hegelianism for Kierkegaard. Thus, the contribution of Kant's Philosophy is twofold. It has occasioned the rise of Romanticism—through Fichte's Philosophy—in the works of the Romantic figures previously discussed. Secondly, as critical Idealism, it is a propadeutic of absolute Idealism that emerges in the Hegelian system.

Indeed, the basis of Kierkegaard's view of Kantianism and the connotation of Modern Philosophy—to reconcile rationality with the infinite—finds expression in Kant's assertion of the moral agent's assertion of God merely as the guarantor of the achievement of the *summum bonum*—the unity of happiness and moral worth. "Christianity is true religion for Kant, not because it gives access to doctrines otherwise hidden from human comprehension, but because alone among the 'public religions' it is in essence a moral religion, which when stripped of its accidental historical and ritual features closely resembles the 'one true religion' in which reside moral principles available to all rational beings."[15] Kierkegaard is critical toward Kantianism because of the reduction of Christianity to a mere system of morality. In *Religion Within the Limits of Reason Alone,* Kant postulates that: "If morality finds in the holiness of its law an object of the greatest respect, then at the level of religion it presents the ultimate cause, which consummates those laws, as an object of adoration and thus appears in its majesty."[16] In this passage, Kant asserts God as the embodiment of the moral laws which emerge in religion under the façade of divinity, as the recipient of worship. God is the set of moral laws that is regarded as divine from the perspective of Christianity. As one commentator observes: "Kierkegaard believes that God is real, but, for some reason, does not do it directly. Kant does it theoretically, by locating the religious in practical reason, whereas Kierkegaard does it through the pseudonymous works."[17]

Kierkegaard thinks that this aspect of Kant's Philosophy is subsequently developed in Kant's Idealist successors and reaches its apex in Hegelianism. Kierkegaard refers to this philosophical orientation as *immanentism*. *Immanentism* is one of the aspects of German Idealism that the *Fragments* sets out implicitly to undermine. *Immanentism* is "the principle that the process of eliminating falsity is tantamount to laying bare the truth, as if falsehood and illogicality were merely impediments to a pre-established capacity to grasp the ultimate nature of things."[18] For Kierkegaard, one of the main issues with German Idealism is the immanentist assumption that removing errors will automatically equip the individual to accept the truth. The German Idealists fail to realize that the truth has to be appropriated subjectively. Kierkegaard thinks that Kantian ethics encroaches upon the boundary between the finite and the infinite. Kierkegaard opposes the deistic view of Kant which situates Christianity strictly in the rational domain. The crux of Kierkegaard's resistance is that the German Idealists removed Christianity from the domain of faith and reduced it to the finite realm of reason. As Hannay observes: "A particularly glaring example of what he [Kierkegaard] considered the misappropriation of religion by Philosophy would be Kant's belief that the essence of Christianity is captured in what we know as morality. This can be called 'immanentism'."[19] From Kierkegaard's perspective, this aspect is problematic in Kant's Philosophy because it transposes Christianity to the domain of practical reasoning and prevents its subjective appropriation by the self.

Another aspect of Kant's Philosophy that Kierkegaard criticizes is the existential implication of the epistemological relation of the self and the *in-itself*. For Kierkegaard, the assertion of the *in-itself* as alien to the *I* represents the failure of Kant's Philosophy to validate existence as such. Although "Both, [Kant and Kierkegaard] are convinced that to receive the empirical manifold means to receive it through what Kant calls 'empirical consciousness', which is most importantly determined by time."[20] Kierkegaard disagrees with the role of existence in Kant's Philosophy. The *in-itself* is not the underlying ground of appearances as

Kant holds, but the expression of existence that Kantianism could not grasp. In the *Postscript,* Climacus points out that one of the weaknesses of Hegel's Philosophy is precisely to have adopted the Kantian account of the relation of the self and *in-itself* and failing to expose Kantianism's inability to acknowledge existence.

> The dubiousness of 'the method' is already apparent in Hegel's relation to Kant. A skepticism that confiscates thinking itself cannot be halted by being thought through, because this must indeed be done by thinking, which is on the side of the mutineer. It must be broken off. To reply to Kant within the fantastical *Shattenspiel* [shadow play] of pure thinking is precisely not to reply to him. -the only *an sich* that cannot be thought is existing, with which thinking has nothing at all to do."

Kantianism bears a skeptic attitude toward existence. Beside, this statement elucidates Kierkegaard's assertion, in the dissertation, that the self remains emaciated in Kant's thought. The self is sterile because existence does not permeate it; in its skeptical relation to the *in-itself* it merely has a superficial connection with actuality through the appearances.

Hegelianism as the Culmination of Modern Philosophy

Kierkegaard's polemic against Hegel is considered by some scholars to be the main drive of his philosophical production. One proponent of this view is Mark Taylor who supports such position in his *Journeys to Selfhood* (2000). The association of Kierkegaard's works with that of Hegel's is so widespread that some scholars, like Mark Taylor, argue that Kierkegaard's project would not have been relevant or conceivable independently of Hegelianism. Although, the question has been raised and debated *ad nauseam*, it is necessary to cast new light on Kierkegaard's attitude toward Hegelianism. Hegel's works and ideas are ubiquitous throughout Kierkegaard's corpus. It is precisely because Hegel's works and ideas are so pervasive in Kierkegaard's texts that to select passages in one text is arbitrary because it implies neglecting the various allusions and discussions of Hegel's thought in the corpus. Thus, the issue is usually solved by being summed up in the position that Kierkegaard was a hostile anti-Hegelian who devoted his authorship to overthrow Hegelianism. However, this is the easy way out. Instead the alternative is to wonder: *Why does Kierkegaard attack Hegel and not Spinoza or a different figure in the History of Philosophy?* The immediate answer is that Hegelianism posits a threat to the self's appropriation of Christianity that is in agreement with the structure of inwardness.

However, the answer to this question remains superficial if one thinks that Kierkegaard is merely challenging Hegelianism when he criticizes Hegel's ideas and texts. The inaccuracy of the claim that Kierkegaard is merely polemical toward Hegel's Philosophy becomes apparent once the following statement is pondered: "On the whole, one has to say that Modern Philosophy, even in its most grandiose forms, nevertheless is really only an introduction to making it possible to philosophize. Hegel undeniably completes—but only the development that had its beginning with Kant and was directed toward knowledge."[22] This claim is pivotal to understand Kierkegaard's view of Hegelianism because it sums up his standpoint on Modern Philosophy and the contribution of Hegel to the development of Modern Philosophy. Kierkegaard thematizes Hegelianism because it is the apex of Modern's Philosophy's attempt to convert Christianity to a phase in world History.

Firstly, it is remarkable that Kierkegaard does not here cite Descartes as the pioneer of Modern Philosophy, but Kant. Kantianism leads the way of Modern Philosophy because Kant holds that the form of subjectivity and the categories are already present in the transcendental subject via the Copernican revolution. It is on the basis of this presupposition that Kierkegaard may claim that Modern Philosophy is an introduction to philosophize. The breakthrough of Kantianism is to have provided autonomy—as the subject's self-awareness and primary role— that is necessary for the epistemological act to occur. In addition, it is not accidental that in the dissertation, Kierkegaard distinguishes Ancient and Modern Irony. In the *Fragments,* Climacus differentiates Ancient and Modern speculation; the former finds expression in the works of Plato and the latter in the works of Schelling and Hegel. Also, Kierkegaard elaborates the distinction between the Ancient and Modern condition in the pamphlet *The Present Age* (1848). The purpose of the frequent demarcation of the Ancient and Modern philosophical discourses in Kierkegaardian corpus is meant to emphasize the transformation that the self undergoes in Modern Philosophy. For Kierkegaard, the gist of Modern Philosophy is to overcome every finite limitation of the subject who ultimately grasps the infinite in thought.

The discussion of Romantic Irony and the role of Fichte as the one who undertakes the next stage of Modern Philosophy shows that Kierkegaard regards German Idealism as a series of philosophical stages that reach their apex in

Hegel's Philosophy. That Kierkegaard regards Schelling's Philosophy as a stage in the evolution of Modern Philosophy is expressed in his view of Schelling's *intellectual intuition*. In the *Postscript,* Climacus asserts that Schelling errs in thinking that the notion of intellectual intuition is an interruption in the circular act of thinking. Schelling fails to realize that intellectual intuition emerges from the depth of self-reflection and is thus in conformity with the Idealist ambition to infinitize the thinking subject. "With regard to thinking's self-reflection, this cannot be said, because, it can keep on for any length of time and runs in circles. Schelling halted self-reflection and understood intellectual intuition not as a discovery within self-reflection that is arrived at by rushing ahead but as a new point of departure. Hegel regards this as a mistake and speaks *absprechend* [deprecatingly] about intellectual intuition—then came the method."[23] Hence, Schelling's Philosophy is a necessary step within the evolution of Modern Philosophy; it is an essential step that anticipates Hegel's methodology.

The implications of Kierkegaard's standpoint on Modern Philosophy show that his polemic toward Hegel cannot strictly be meant toward Hegelianism. Kierkegaard is critical of the attempt of Modern Philosophy—to reconcile the finitude of thought with the infinite aspect of Christianity—that reaches its completion in Hegel's Philosophy. In the corpus, Kierkegaard is critiquing both, Modern Philosophy and Hegelianism. Hegel is the object of Kierkegaard's polemic because it is the zenith of Modern Philosophy; Hegelianism is the ultimate outcome of Modern Philosophy.

It is through continuous engagement with the German Idealists that Kierkegaard's heritage in this tradition becomes obvious. Kierkegaard's philosophical project stands as a critical reflection upon the ambition of Modern Philosophy. Careful consideration of Kierkegaardian thought suggests that it is attempting to show the impossibility of the ambition of the Idealists to dovetail the finite difference of the subject with the eternal essence of Christianity in thought. According to Kierkegaard, the irrational reality that Hegel believes he makes meaningful for the self through mediation is the absurdity of the Christian way of life. On the other hand, Kierkegaard strives to maintain the distinction between the rational faculties and the absurdity of Christianity by positing it as an impervious paradox to thought. The *Philosophical Fragments* and the *Concluding Unscientific Postscript* represent the mature philosophical expression of Kierkegaard's attempt to show that the historical knower cannot achieve the eternal happiness of Christianity by the means of the rational faculties. In these texts, Kierkegaard is engaging with the philosophical discourses of Hegel's predecessors and Hegelianism. It is by so doing that Kierkegaard partakes in the tradition of Modern Philosophy. The uniformity of the two texts offers a critique of Modern Philosophy and brings forth Kierkegaard's inclination toward a Post-Modern experience of religion.

Climacus's *Philosophical Fragments*

This section of the project is the first part of a twofold aim which is to establish the autonomy of Kierkegaard's Philosophy while drawing out the influences of German Idealism and Romanticism in the formulation of Kierkegaard's main concepts in the *Philosophical Fragments* and *Concluding Unscientific Postscript*. It is going to focus primarily on the first of these two books. The following chapter will carry out the second phase by focusing on *Concluding Unscientific Postscript*. The attempt to draw out the self-sufficiency of Kierkegaard's philosophical project has to consider the philosophic-theological queries that it sets out to address. Only then will it become evident that the autonomy of Kierkegaard's Philosophy depends primarily on critiquing Modern Philosophy and Romanticism. This is the first part of Climacus's attempt to answer the question: *Can eternal happiness be achieved on the basis of History?*

The selection of *Philosophical Fragments* and *Concluding Unscientific Postscript* for the purpose of the investigation is due to the fact that they represent the most consistent expositions of Kierkegaard's philosophical and theological views. In these two mature works, Kierkegaard is pondering the relationship of History and eternal happiness. The rigorous investigation of these two themes that animate most of Kierkegaard's corpus is consummated in these works. The above consideration of Kierkegaard's engagement with the Idealist and Romantic notions is conducive to understand these two texts because Kierkegaard relies on his assessment of the Romantic view of Irony and the philosophical discourses of the Idealists to develop the essential categories of *Philosophical Fragments* and *Concluding Unscientific Postscript*.

The structure of the project thus follows two methodological approaches. The first method of our investigation is oriented toward an immanent interpretation of the *Fragments* and *Concluding Unscientific Postscript*. The immanent approach to Kierkegaard's two texts is meant to draw out the intrinsic unity of the views that the pseudonymous author wishes to put forth. In compliance with Kierkegaard's request not to conflate the claims of the pseudonymous authorship with his own, the immanent approach allows the pseudonymous author to delineate his position without imposing any external and arbitrary views on the text. Under the light of the immanent interpretation, the texts can stand autonomously and the philosophical arguments that they put forth may emerge according to the inner dynamics that underlie them. The second method supplements the first one. The philosophical-historical is intended to make explicit the implicit references of the pseudonymous author to the Idealist and Romantic concepts. The philosophical-historical is meant to set up the broader philosophical horizon of the author's argument. Also, it accentuates the participation of the texts within the Idealist and Romantic traditions. The analysis of the *Philosophical Fragments* is exegetical in following each section judiciously in order to be loyal to Johannes Climacus's development of the philosophical ground for the arguments of the subsequent *Concluding Unscientific Postscript*. On the basis of the thorough development of the first work, it will be feasible to focus upon the essential arguments of the *CUP* since it is beyond the expected length of this project to elaborate every section of Kierkegaard's mammoth piece.

Moreover, the exegesis of each text will be loyal to the deliberate ironical structure of Johannes Climacus's exposition. The Irony consists in the fact that in spite of its small appearance, the *Fragments* is the condensation of the theoretical notions that Climacus relies on in the attempt to answer the question: *Can Eternal Happiness be Built on Historical Knowledge?* It is thus in agreement with Climacus's ironical approach that the development of the *Fragments* will be longer than that of the same issue—under historical costume—in the *CUP*. Unpacking the complex notions of the *Fragments* and their implicit aspects is more demanding in both, length and philosophical attention. The disparity in the presentation of the two texts is faithful to the pseudonymous nature of Johannes Climacus. The ironic and humoristic nature of Johannes Climacus will be further developed at the end of the exegesis of the *CUP*.

Greek Recollection and the Moment

The *Preface* of the *Philosophical Fragments* begins with an emphasis upon the humble ambition of the work. Climacus designates it as a *pamphlet*. The purpose of Climacus's accentuation upon the *Fragment*, as a limited undertaking, is twofold; it is meant to be ironic and also to demarcate the work in relation to systematic philosophical endeavors. Climacus's designation of the text as a *pamphlet* is meant to express his ironical attitude toward systematic Philosophy. Also, it is noteworthy that Climacus selects the title, *Philosophical Fragments,* and qualifies the project as a *pamphlet* to point out its discontinuous nature. Climacus wishes to distinguish it from the works of systematic philosophers, which strive to establish continuity in their investigation. The first statement of the text is ironic and announces Climacus's critical attitude toward systematic philosophical discourses. "What is offered here is only a pamphlet, *proprio Marte, propriis auspiciis, proprio stipendio* [by one's own hand, on one's own behalf, at one's own expense], without any claim to being part of the scientific-scholarly endeavor..."[1] For Climacus, systematic Philosophy complies with the requirements of scientific projects. Climacus introduces implicitly the dichotomy between *pamphlet* and *scientific-scholarly* texts, which is going to be the basis of his critique of systematic Philosophy. "And of course it is impossible for anyone to dream of attributing world-historical importance to a pamphlet (something that I, at least, regard as the greatest danger that could threaten my undertaking) or to assume that its author is the systematic Salomon Goldkab so long awaited in our dear capital city, Copenhagen."[2] In this ironic claim, Climacus directly asserts the non-systematic and non-historical intentions of the text.

The incentive for the non-scholarly nature of the work derives from the fact that the author wishes to avoid the inherent rigidity of systematic philosophical discourses. Climacus wants the text to unfold on the basis of intellectual flexibility. The cognitive faculties should be put at the service of the object of thought instead of attempting to dominate it. This approach allows the issue to reveal itself freely to thought. This fact is apparent in Climacus's denial of any philosophical opinion, which usually serves as the guiding thread of philosophical text. "To have an opinion is to me both, too much and too little;"[3] The problematic aspect of having an opinion is later revealed when Climacus states his wish to remain flexible toward the affairs of the spirit: "In the world of spirit, this is my case, for I have trained myself and am training myself always to be able to dance lightly in the service of thought,"⁴ Climacus's metaphor discloses the author's disposition to follow the rhythm of the issues under consideration by thought.

Then, Climacus proceeds to assert the philosophical authority of the work on its existential basis. The existential grounding represents Climacus's alternative to the systematic basis of the philosophical works of the Idealists. The text is going to develop upon the existential experiences of the thinker instead of the domination of the cognitive faculties in dealing with the issues at hand. "The whole book can be seen as an extended discussion paper of the qualification required for a teacher of existence."⁵ Furthermore, the effectiveness of the *Philosophical Fragments* rests on both, the philosophical issues and their relevance to Climacus's existence. Climacus emphasizes the importance of an existential transformation by making it crucial for spiritual improvement. "I can stake my own life, I can in all earnestness trifle with my own life—not with another's."⁶ Through this claim, Climacus weaves his pseudonymous nature with the issues under investigation. Climacus's statement seems to be an indirect invitation to the reader to contemplate the existential aspect of his philosophical project.

In addition, Climacus uses the first person perspective to address the individual reader and not the neutral position of a scholarly project. It is noteworthy that Climacus ends the *CUP* with a direct address to the reader as well. Climacus reinforces that his priority is not systematic correctness, but existential experience through the statement that he overcomes intellectual difficulty with his life and not with learning since he has none to offer. "All I have is my life, which I promptly stake every time a difficulty appears. Then it is easy to dance, for the thought of death is a good dancing partner, my dancing partner. Every human being is too heavy for me,"⁷ Climacus is here anticipating the disposition of the subjective thinker that is going to be developed under 'historical costume' in the *CUP*. For Climacus, the existential thinker ought to reflect alone under the light of her existential experiences; to attempt to think for others is presumptuous and posits an onus for any thinker.

A

The underlying tone of the *Preface* is renewed in the motto of the first chapter of the text in which Climacus feigns thorough ignorance of the motive for the question at stake. He asserts the following in the form of a proposition: "The question is asked by one who in his ignorance does not even know what provided the occasion for his questioning in this way."⁸ This proposition sheds light upon Climacus's disposition, which is free of all preconceived notions. Climacus is proceeding according to the intrinsic necessity to address the issue; the exposition is occasioned by the issue itself. Climacus reveals his pseudonymous nature as the unbiased mouthpiece of the driving questions of the exposition. This fact will be further developed at the end of the *Postscript.* In the first chapter of the *Philosophical Fragments,* Climacus sets out to address the question: *Can the truth be learned?* However, the puzzling aspect of this endeavor is that Climacus himself states that he is ignorant of the circumstance, which occasions the question. In a previous draft, Climacus asserts the historical ground of the question: "One in ignorance who presumably knows historically what he is asking about but seeks the answer.—*Pap.* 5 B10 *n.d.,* 1844"[9] The historical ground lies in the fact that the question is raised in a temporal context. Although Climacus claims to be ignorant of the specific incentive of the question, he acknowledges that it has emerged from his temporal circumstances.

Climacus, then, introduces the guideline of the question, which is Socratic by nature. The feigning of ignorance is elucidated by Climacus's reference to the epistemological issue of Plato's *Meno.* Climacus presents Socrates's argument that it is impossible to search for what one already knows since such pursuit would be futile. On the other hand, one cannot set out to search for what one does not know since the searcher would not even be able to recognize what is sought. The sole alternative is thus *recollection,* according to which knowing is the appropriation of what is latent within the knower. Hence Climacus establishes Platonic recollection as the paradigm of his analysis of the question: *Can the truth be learned?*

> Socrates thinks through the difficulty by means [of the principle] that all learning and seeking are but recollecting. Thus the ignorant person merely needs to be reminded in order, by himself, to call to mind what he knows. The truth is not introduced into him but was in him.[10]

Platonic recollection is fundamental to the overall structure of Climacus's exposition. This fact is evident in the conscientious manner that Climacus elaborates upon it. Climacus argues that recollection underlies the Hellenic notion of the immortality and pre-existence of the soul. "Socrates elaborates on this idea, and in it the Greek pathos is in fact concentrated, since it becomes a demonstration for the immortality of the soul—retrogressively, please note—or a demonstration for the pre-existence of the soul."[11] For Climacus, in order for recollection to take place, the soul as the bearer of that which is to be recollected must pre-exist and persist after physical death. It is upon the basis of this theme that Climacus elaborates the Ancient and Modern views of the eternal. For Climacus, recollection is always implicit in the Ancient and Modern views of Eternity because of the amalgamation of the 'pre' and the 'post', which makes up the continuity of the eternal.

> an eternal creating, an eternal emanating from the father, an eternal becoming of the deity, an eternal self-sacrifice, a past resurrection, a judgment over and done with. All these ideas are that Greek idea of recollection, although this is not always noticed, because they have been arrived at by going further. If the idea is analyzed in a tallying of the various states of pre-existence, then the eternal 'pre's' of that approximating thinking are similar to the eternal 'post's' of the corresponding approximation."

Although Climacus develops this argument in a footnote and the account of the eternal that it provides manifests itself implicitly throughout the text. The point is that the eternal consists in the continuity of the 'pre's' and 'post's' and is not subject to any temporal interruption. Climacus is setting up the ground for the contrast between the eternal and historical, which is to follow.

For Climacus, Socrates is meritorious for having been disposed consistently as a midwife assisting the birth of ideas. Socrates's midwifery or the *maieutic* method is commendable because Socrates always adheres to it in his dialogical relation to his interlocutors. For Climacus, "He was and continued to be a midwife, not because he 'did not have the positive,' but because he perceived that this relation is the highest relation a human being can have to another."[13] Besides, the consistent aspect of the midwife relation is worthy in virtue of the fact that it is a relation between two individuals, which has its starting point in a subjective relationship. "And in that he is indeed forever right, for even if a divine point of departure is ever given, this remains the true relation between one human being and another"[14] The relation of the midwife, which Socrates exemplifies, is the paradigmatic relation throughout the Kierkegaardian corpus. Thus, consistent reference to Socratic *maieutic* in the two texts is due to the fact that it illustrates a subjective relation, which is not mediated by any system of thought. Rather, the subjective starting point provides the guiding rules. In addition, the birth of the idea does not come from Socrates or the interlocutor as singularities, but subjective exchange allows the idea to come about via the interaction of Socrates and the questioner. "because between one human being and another μαιεύεσθαι [to deliver] is the highest; giving birth indeed belongs to the god."[15]

For Climacus, the genuine process of philosophizing should comply with the *maieutic* method, as well. In such context, the teacher or philosopher assists the questioner in the elucidation of the issue at stake. Authentic Philosophy is thus not the academic enterprise in which learned individuals exchange ideas, but makes it possible—with divine assistance—for the questioner to reach the truth. This fact is apparent in Climacus's emphasis upon the humane aspect of Socrates's approach. "This is the profundity of Socratic thinking, this his noble, thoroughgoing humanity, which does not exclusively and conceitedly cultivate the company of brilliant minds but...philosophized just as absolutely with whomever he spoke."[16] Unlike the model of systematic thinking, the Socratic way posits the individual above the idea. Socratic midwifery considers the individual as the pivotal aspect in the development of the idea. "In the Socratic view, every human being is himself the midpoint, and the whole world focuses only on him because his self-knowledge is God-knowledge."[17] Climacus establishes an isomorphic link between the subjective and divine relation. In the process of giving birth to the idea there is syncretism of the divine and the human. This isomorphic relation sets up the platform for the discussion of the issue of eternal happiness and History, which appears under the form of the divine and the human.

The exchange between the instructor and the questioner grants priority to the rise of truth instead of making the instructor's authority absolute. Climacus uses Socratic recollection to illustrate the accidental nature of the historical point at which one appropriates the truth because the truth was always latent in the learner. The process of instruction takes place in the temporal domain of the historical. Its purpose is to occasion the rise of the truth, which was concealed in the questioner. "Neither can the fact that the teaching of Socrates or of Prodicus was this or that have anything but historical interest for me, because the truth in which I rest was in me and emerged from me."[18] The fact that the truth has always been latent in the learner makes the historical juncture at which it emerges accidental. On the other hand, the truth is absolute because it constitutes the source of the individual's eternal happiness. Its absolute nature derives from the fact that it allows the individual to transcend the historical process of instruction. "My relation to Socrates and Prodicus cannot concern me with regard to my eternal happiness, for this is given retrogressively in the possession of the truth that I had from the beginning without knowing it."[19] The temporal point at which the learner awakens the truth brings about the insight that one has always had it. Also, this temporal event is absorbed in the eternal because it derives its worth from its eternal origin.

The reason for Climacus's preference for Socratic midwifery, as the ideal relation, is gradually becoming evident. Midwifery represents the intersection between the historical and the eternal; it provides the historical ladder upon which the individual may climb toward the eternal. The divine aspect of this relation makes itself manifest in the historical in order to raise the individual to the awareness of the eternal. For Climacus: "The temporal point of departure is nothing, because in the same moment I discover that I have known the truth from Eternity without knowing it, in the same instant that moment is hidden in the eternal,"[20]

The time of the acquisition of the truth is transforming in two ways. It is a rupture of the historical, which allows the truth to emerge. Also, it allows the individual to acknowledge her eternal nature.

B

Climacus, then, introduces the *moment* as a central theme of the text whose significance consists in its transforming role. The meaningfulness of the *moment* lies in its ability to interrupt the historical and allowing the individual to acknowledge eternal truth. Climacus defines the moment in a separate paragraph: "If the situation is to be different, then the moment in time must have such decisive significance that for no moment will I be able to forget it, neither in time nor Eternity, because the eternal, previously nonexistent, came into existence in that moment."[21] Climacus posits the *moment* as a working hypothesis, which is yet to be proven. The *moment* is to derive its autonomy after reflecting upon the state of the learner before the rise of truth and its impact upon the learner after truth has come about.

Climacus anticipates a difficulty that may undermine the central role of the *moment*. According to his rationale, the Socratic dilemma about the status of the truth in the learner prior to the act of recollection is overcome by the awakening of the truth that was latent in the learner. However, such awareness undermines the importance of the *moment*, which comes to stand as the mere occasion for what was latent to become manifest. For Climacus, what is at stake is that the *moment* acquires the function of a mere externality, which only occasions an inner event, but does not have any autonomous status. To address this issue, Climacus formulates a new premise. "Now if the moment is to acquire decisive significance, then the seeker up until that moment must not have possessed the truth, not even in the form of ignorance, for in that case the moment becomes merely the moment of occasion; indeed, he must not even be a seeker."[22] The importance of this new premise revolves upon the word 'possessed' that is meant to emphasize the appropriation of subjective truth. To 'possess' the truth thus acquires an existential characteristic. Climacus associates truth and existential experience in the following claim, where he deliberately uses the copula 'is' instead of 'has'. "Consequently, he has to be defined as being outside the truth (not coming toward it like a proselyte, but going away from it) or as untruth. He *is*, then, untruth."[23] The self is not outside the truth as one who has been excluded and is moving toward it, but as one who was in truth and moved away from it. The truth is the center from which the self is alienated.

The question: *how does one who is untruth come to be in truth?* brings along a new theme, mainly, the *teacher*. The role of the *teacher* is determined primarily by the state of the learner prior to the rise of truth. The *teacher* may not assist the learner in recollecting the truth because she is merely untruth. Thus the role of the *teacher*'s instruction is to help the learner to realize that she is untruth. "Consequently, in this way, precisely by reminding him, the teacher thrusts the learner away, except that by being turned in upon himself in this manner the learner does not discover that he previously knew the truth but discovers his untruth."[24] In this passage Climacus suggests that to be aware that one is untruth does not represent an intellectual inadequacy, but an existential plight. Climacus elaborates both, the epistemological role of the *teacher*, who complies with the dynamic of Socratic midwifery and the existential realization of untruth. He claims that: "To this act of consciousness, the Socratic principle applies: the teacher is only an occasion whoever he may be, even if he is a god, because I can discover my own untruth only by myself"[25] The *teacher*'s role becomes manifold since the instruction, the truth, which she is supposed to transmit requires not merely the ability to understand on the part of the learner, but an existential disposition as well.

The second role of the teacher is to give the learner the condition to understand the truth. According to Climacus, the acquisition of the condition is mandatory because otherwise the learner would only have to will to recollect the truth. The condition is the act of asking about the truth. To inquire about the truth is the initial act, which extricates the learner from her state of untruth. For Climacus, the question about the truth and the condition are concurrent.

> Along with it, he must provide him with the condition for understanding it, for if the learner were himself the condition for understanding the truth, then he merely needs to recollect, because the condition for understanding the truth is like being able to ask about it—the condition and the question contain the conditioned and the answer.[26]

Part of the teacher's role is to occasion the rise of the question. It is only upon the fulfillment of the condition that the teacher may undertake the task of teaching. In accordance with the learner's situation, the teacher has to bring her to undergo a metamorphosis. Hence the teacher's method differs from epistemological teaching, which aims at reformation: "Ultimately, all instruction depends upon the presence of the condition; if it is lacking, then a teacher is capable of nothing, because in the second case, the teacher, before beginning to teach, must transform, not reform the learner."[27] It is because of this unearthly task that Climacus asserts that in order for the teacher to carry out the transformation he has to be the *god*. "But no human being is capable of doing this; if it is to take place, it must be done by the god himself."[28] Climacus arrives at the solution of the issue regarding the undermining of the significance of the *moment* by positing it as the occurrence of the acquisition of the condition. "But insofar as the moment is to have decisive significance (and if this is not assumed, then we do in fact remain with the Socratic), he must lack the condition, consequently be deprived of it."[29] By intensifying the existential predicament of the learner, which is stretched beyond intellectual necessity, Climacus also alters the status of the teacher. The existential situation of the learner demands more than mere intellectual guidance.

Climacus raises the role of the *teacher* from the human position of the Socratic midwife relation to a divine status. The state of untruth and the fact that the learner deviated from the truth willingly constitutes *sin*. For Climacus, it is the state of unfreedom that the learner has brought upon herself. Also, it is essential to the functions of the teacher to make the learner responsible for her sinful state. "In speaking of 'the god' Climacus thus manages to adopt an initially neutral stance with respect to the two hypotheses, while at the same time provoking thought about the relationship between Socrates's god and the god of the religions hypothesis."[30] It is such ambiguous presentation of the god that makes the transition from Socrates to the Christian experience possible. The finite nature of the teacher is therefore inadequate to carry out this deed. Climacus expresses this fact when he raises the following question: "Now, what should we call such a teacher, for we surely agree that we have gone far beyond the definition of a teacher."[31] Climacus justifies the alteration of the *teacher* indirectly through the existential necessity of the learner, which requires divine intervention. The existential predicament of the learner, which is expressed through her need for the condition calls for a divine teacher. In Climacus's words:

> The teacher, then, is the god himself, who, acting as the occasion, prompts the learner to be reminded that he is untruth and is that through his own fault. But this state—to be untruth and to be that through one's own fault—what can we call it? Let us call it *sin*.[32]

The fact that the teacher can free the learner from the bondage of sin and lead her toward the truth is the basis of his status as the savior. The teacher is the savior in virtue of the ability to assist in freeing the learner from sin. The existential predicament of the learner in the state of untruth makes divine intervention necessary in order to overcome *sin*. The *teacher* is thus the only means for the learner's restoration to freedom. Climacus stresses the crucial role of the *teacher* vis-à-vis the learner through several labels. *Savior, deliverer,* and *reconciler* represent the different functions that the *teacher* performs in order to set the learner free from unfreedom. "Let us call him a *savior*, for he does indeed save the learner from unfreedom, saves him from himself. Let us call him a *deliverer*, for he does indeed deliver the person who had imprisoned himself...and if that teacher gives him the condition and the truth, then he is, of course, a *reconciler* who takes away the wrath that lay over the incurred guilt."³³ It is in virtue of these functions that the *teacher* becomes unforgettable to the learner.

At this juncture of the text, Climacus seems to presuppose the reader to be familiar with *Vigilius Haufniensis*'s account of the occurrence of original *sin* and the ensuing Fall, which is developed in the psychological-dogmatic exposition of the *Concept of Anxiety*. Furthermore, by positing the need for divine intervention, Climacus indirectly points out the insufficiency of the Hellenic solution to ignorance. Climacus shows that the Socratic *teacher* as finite is not fit to help remedy ignorance, which he is pondering from the Christian perspective as an existential defect that only providence may remove. Climacus's account of the condition, as an existential inadequacy, or *sin* is similar to the ignorance that causes anxiety. As this description of ignorance, in the *Concept of Anxiety*, shows: the *teacher* of Socratic midwifery is unfit to cure it.

> Innocence is ignorance. In innocence, man is not qualified as spirit but is psychically qualified in immediate unity with his natural condition. The spirit in man is dreaming...In this state there is peace and repose, but there is simultaneously something else that is not contention and strife, for there is indeed nothing against which to strive. What, then, is it? Nothing. But what effect does nothing have? It begets anxiety.³⁴

To return to Climacus's discussion of the moment, it is the learner's need of the condition that makes the *moment* significant because it is through it that the subjective transformation happens. The state of untruth represents an existential state, which like *sin* is the outcome of the individual's choice. The unfreedom that follows from the learner's choice is the source of the state of untruth and the need of the condition. Climacus discusses the relation between freedom and unfreedom in a footnote, in which he compares the choice of unfreedom to that of a child who decides to purchase a toy instead of a book. "And so it was also once, when man could buy freedom and unfreedom for the same price, and this price was the free choice of the soul and the surrender of the choice. He chose unfreedom,"³⁵ Just as the child is unable to exchange the toy for a book; the learner cannot easily forsake the state of untruth by simply willing it. According to Climacus, the learner's impotence to will herself out untruth is due to the fact that she has been confined to the state of *sin* by unfreedom. "(And this is truly just the way it is, for he uses the power of freedom in the service of unfreedom, since he is indeed freely in it, and in this way the combined power of unfreedom grows and makes him the slave of sin.)"[36]

The transformation that the learner undergoes after receiving the condition and the truth makes her a follower. Climacus characterizes the learner as a follower in order to express the qualitative change and difference in orientation that occurred in the subjectivity of the learner. Climacus links the experience of the follower to the act of conversion which has a Christian connotation in the following:

> Inasmuch as he was untruth, he was continually in the process of departing from the truth; as a result of receiving the condition in the moment, his course took the opposite direction, or he was turned around. Let us call this change *conversion,* even though this is a word hitherto unused; but we choose it precisely in order to avoid confusion, for it seems to be created for the very change of which we speak.[37]

The *follower* is the prototype of the subjective state of the learner after the acquisition of the condition in the moment. This state contributes to demonstrate the necessity and meaningfulness of the moment that Climacus established previously as a working hypothesis to be proven. It substantiates the moment because the transition from not being to being has taken place via the moment.

Climacus discusses the unforgettable role of the teacher, which is linked to the moment. Climacus redeems the initial historical point of the relation by positing the teacher as unforgettable, which in turn makes the *moment,* as a temporal entity, equally unforgettable. Climacus restores the historical aspect in order to secure the temporal basis of the manifestation of the eternal. "Even when the teacher has most fully put on the condition and then, by doing so, has become immersed in the truth, he still can never forget that teacher or allow him to disappear Socratically."[38] It is remarkable that it is only after establishing the unforgettable role of the teacher that Climacus asserts the uniqueness of the moment, which represents the *fullness* of time. "And, now, the moment. A moment such as this is unique…A moment such as this must have a special name. Let us call it: *the fullness of time.*"[39] Moreover, Climacus's characterization of the moment as the fullness of time is meant to demonstrate its validity as a working hypothesis in addressing the question: *can the truth be learned?*

There are two underlying themes in Climacus's exposition. Climacus develops the Hellenic theme by positing Socrates as the exemplar for teaching the truth. Climacus deliberately links Socrates with the historical because the *maieutic* method is intended to point out the need for a higher intervention. This fact shows the necessity of the Hellenic standpoint as an inescapable starting point, and indicates its impotence when confronted with the existential circumstance of the learner. Thus, Climacus starts with the Hellenic tradition via Socrates in order to transcend the Socratic and introduce the Christian moment. This fact shows that the transcendence of the Hellenic tradition is, for Climacus, necessary to prepare the ground for the Christian experience. Thus, Hong observes correctly that: "Going beyond Socrates in *Fragments* thus becomes an elaboration of the first thesis in *The Concept of Irony*."[40] The development of Socratic Irony through the analysis of the various accounts of Socrates's life and deeds makes up the first thesis. Climacus is striving to go beyond Socratic Irony to show the necessity of the Christian disposition.

Moreover, Climacus's use of the Hellenic tradition, as the starting point of his project, suggests his Romantic heritage. The fact that Climacus asserts Socrates as the ideal teacher is not an accidental fact. It was characteristic of the Romantic writers to dwell on the experiences of the Greeks as exemplars for the Modern individual. Climacus's reverence for Socrates suggests that he partakes in the longing for Greek civilization that was an essential feature of the Romantic writers. More specifically, the frequent appeals to Socrates throughout Kierkegaardian corpus is reminding of Friedrich Schlegel's admiration for the Greeks. The reference to Schlegel is legitimate because Kierkegaard had read Schlegel's works intensively and reproduced the attitude of Schlegel's protagonist in *Lucinde* in the character of the seducer in *Either/Or*. In addition, Kierkegaard devoted a section of his dissertation, *The Concept of Irony* to the analysis of Schlegel's view of Irony. According to Hannay, Kierkegaard was influenced by the Romantic attitude toward the Greeks and shared the political position of Schlegel among other Romantics, as well:

> Both, Friedrich Schlegel (1772-1829) and Novalis (1772-1801) praised Robespierre's passionate and consistent dedication to the ideal of freedom, and both, were engrossed in Fichte's Idealism, though they later criticized the Terror on the one hand and Fichte's one-sided intellectualism on the other. The conclusion we might draw is that by this time Kierkegaard's own views accorded with these criticisms.[41]

The influence of the Romantics is manifest in both, the ironic attitude of the *Preface* and the first part of the *Fragments*. Besides, the privileged role of the Greeks can be traced in Schlegel's works as well. In the following statement, Frank offers evidence of Schlegel's high regard for the Greeks: "And second of all, it was Friedrich Schlegel himself whose thought is especially rooted in the foundational works of the classical epoch generally and in the classical period of art in particular; it was with reference to Schlegel that the satirical term 'Graecomania' was invented by Karl Phillip Moritz, I think."⁴⁸ Thus, the role of Socrates in Climacus's account is an expression of the influence of the Romantics. The influence of Romanticism emerges throughout the text as it progresses.

The Historical Manifestation of the Divine

The second chapter begins with a consideration and appraisal of Socrates and Socratic midwifery. Climacus structures the first paragraph to express the *autopathetic-sympathetic* nature of Socrates's relation to those who learn from him. The basis of this relation is the finite situation of both, Socrates and the learner that assures the isomorphic exchange between them. For Climacus, it is in virtue of the circumstances of Socrates's life that he was able to relate to those of the learner in his attempt to provide guidance. Thus, the dynamic of the relation, according to Climacus, is such that Socrates's teaching, which aims at influencing the learner, represents the opportunity for Socrates to be influenced by the learner as well. "Understood in this way—and this was indeed the Socratic understanding—the teacher stands in a mutual relation, inasmuch as life and its situations are the occasion for him to become a teacher and he in turn the occasion for others to learn something. His relation, therefore, is at all times marked by autopathy just as much as by sympathy."⁴⁹ The rewarding aspect of the *autopathetic- sympathetic* teaching is the mutual influence of the two parties upon each other. Furthermore, this relation is consistent with Climacus's previous position that the learner does not make the teacher absolute, and the learner does not become dependable upon the teacher.

Climacus distinguishes the god, as the divine teacher, from Socrates, as the Hellenic teacher. The difference consists in the fact that Socrates as the finite teacher was moved by a call to take up his function as teacher of the youth in Athens. Socrates's vocation lies within the finite in which he assumes his teaching role as a response to the historical situation of his time. On the other hand, the god, as the divine teacher, is not compelled by any external event to give the condition. The god, in contradistinction to Socrates, is brought to teach by an intrinsic necessity. Climacus cites Aristotle's definition of the unmoved mover in the *Metaphysics* as the paradigm of the dynamics of the god as the divine teacher: "But the god needs no pupil in order to understand himself, and no occasion can act upon him in such a way that there is just as much in the occasion as in the resolution. What, then, moves him to make his appearance? He must move himself and continue to be what Aristotle says of him αχινητος παντα χινει [unmoved he moves all]"⁴⁴ The god is the ideal teacher because the genesis and telos for assuming his teaching task lie within him. Climacus elaborates this fact and posits love as that from which the god derives the drive to assist the learner. "But if he moves himself and is not moved by need, what moves him then but love, for love does not have the satisfaction of need outside itself but within."⁴⁵ Climacus's position here reveals the influence of Aristotelian metaphysics upon his project. Indeed, as one commentator observes, Aristotelian logic plays an important role in Kierkegaard's corpus:

> The way in which Kierkegaard describes the movements of the individual from possibility to actuality, the intimate relationship between possibility and freedom, qualitative change in human life, etc., is indebted to his own interpretation of central notions in Aristotle's thought as seen through the prism of Trendelenburg's Aristotelian studies.⁴⁶

That Climacus wishes to use the Socratic and at the same time to transcend it is obvious in the following statement about the god and the moment:

> His resolution, which does not have an equal reciprocal relation to the occasion, must be from Eternity, even though, fulfilled in time, it expressly becomes *the moment*, for where the occasion and what is occasioned correspond equally, as equally as to the reply to the shout in the desert, the moment does not appear but is swallowed by recollection into its Eternity. The moment emerges precisely in the relation of the eternal resolution to the unequal occasion. If this is not the case, then we return to the Socratic and do not have the god or the eternal resolution or the moment.⁴⁷

The relation of the eternal and temporal, which occurs through the expression of the god's love toward the historical individual, is made manifest in the *moment*. Climacus means the metaphor of the shout in the desert to suggest the intersection of the eternal and History in the occurrence of the *moment*. In addition, Climacus links the Greek notion of recollection with the Christian notion of Eternity. The moment is the juncture at which the temporal is commensurable with its eternal origin.

Climacus proceeds in such a way that the eternal is reconciled with the temporal via the moment, and the eternal nature of the god is reconciled with temporality through love. Love represents the equalizer that overcomes the ontological difference between the finite learner and the infinite god. "The love, then, must be for the learner, and the goal must be to win him, for only in love is the different made equal, and only in equality or in unity is there understanding."[48] However, a difficulty arises in the love relation of the god and the learner. The attempt to overcome the ontological difference between the two parties runs the risk of violating the finitude of the learner. Climacus wants to preserve the dignity of the learner as a finite entity in the face of the infinite god. This difficulty reveals Climacus's subtle allusion to Jesus Christ's dilemma to describe his nature to his disciples while displaying respect for their human frailty. Climacus is aiming at bridging the gap of History with the infinite nature of the god who personifies Christ.

Climacus characterizes this difficulty as a problem of mutual understanding between the teacher and the learner. "Yet this love is basically unhappy, for they are very unequal, and what seems so easy—namely, that the god must be able to make himself understood—is not so easy if he is not to destroy that which is different."[49] This difficulty opens up two plausible solutions. The first one consists in elevating the human learner to divine status. However, Climacus refutes this alternative because it would be deceiving and offensive to the learner's finite situation: "In his [god's] own eyes, just to express his love incompletely would be a deception, even if no one understood him, even if reproach sought to vex his soul."[50] Moreover, this deed would do away with the significance of the moment, since the rise of the truth would not take place in time; the moment would be absorbed in infinity. Hence Climacus wishes to salvage both, the learner's finitude and the meaningfulness of the moment. Assuming the perspective of the god, Climacus claims: "But if the moment is to have decisive significance, how unutterable his concern becomes!"[51]

The second alternative is the descent of the god into the temporal sphere of History. This option is illustrated through the *maieutic* attitude of Socratic teaching, which assumes ignorance in order to guide the learner toward the truth. In Socratic teaching, love for the learner is cloaked under ignorance. "Therefore, the unity must be brought about in some other way. Here we are once again mindful of Socrates, for what else was his ignorance but the unitive expression of love for the learner?"[52] However, Socratic teaching is limited. For Climacus, it may only prepare the stage for thoughts regarding the beautiful to be born. Socratic teaching appeals only to the application of the rational faculties and recollection. The limitation is that Socratic teaching is confined to speech about finite matters. Socrates is a mere midwife and may not give birth himself.

> Between one human being and another, to be of assistance is supreme, but to beget is reserved for the god, whose love is *procreative*, but not that procreative love of which Socrates knew how to speak so beautifully on festive occasion.

> Such a love does not mark the relation of the teacher to the pupil but the relation of the autodidact to the beautiful as he, ignoring dispersed beauty, envisions beauty-in-and-by-itself and now gives birth to many beautiful and glorious discourses and thoughts"[53]

The love that Climacus is discussing is divine by nature because it is essentially able to birth the transformation of the learner.

The god must manifest himself in the most abject and powerless position. Climacus asserts the function of a servant as the ideal character for the god to assume in order to avoid offending the historical and finite circumstance of the learner. "In order for unity to be effected, the god must become like this one. He will appear, therefore, as the equal of the lowliest of persons. But the lowliest of all is one who must serve others—consequently, the god will appear in the form of a *servant.*"[54] The god's role as a servant is not a social function that he fulfills at given times. For Climacus, the god's embrace of the role of the servant is intrinsic and inalienable to his nature. "But the form of the servant was not something put on. Therefore the god must suffer all things, endure all things be tried in all things, hunger in the desert, thirst in his agonies, be forsaken in death, absolutely the equal of the lowliest of human beings"[55] The tribulation of the god under human form is inevitable. For Climacus, the god must endure the most humiliating aspects of humanity. The pain of the human form must pervade the being of the god so completely that it is only in death that it can be forsaken. "But the form of the servant was not something put on, and therefore he must expire in death and in turn leave the earth."[56] The expression of love becomes manifest through suffering. The suffering of love assures the authentic humanity of the god. Climacus posits suffering as the means through which the god fully relinquishes the privilege of his divine station.

Furthermore, the descent of the god into the human realm bears a tremendous consequence for the human learner. Climacus situates the impact of the god's descent in the faculty of the understanding of the learner. Unlike the god, the learner does not undergo physical alteration, as a result of the descent, but is initially affected through the understanding. "And the situation of understanding—in its frailty, how close it is at every moment to the border of misunderstanding when the anxieties of guilt disturb the peace of love."[57] Climacus is anticipating the clash of the understanding with the fact that the god has put on a human costume. The reaction of the understanding as it grapples with the historical presence of the divine is going to be the thesis of the next chapter.

Climacus concludes this section with some reflections upon the reader's reaction to his account. In agreement with the title of the exposition as a poetic venture, Climacus comments upon the poem and the undertaking of the poet:

> Or is this poem perhaps like a proverb, of which no author is known because it seems as if all humanity had composed it. And was this perhaps why you called my plagiarism the shabbiest ever, because I did not steal from any one person but robbed the human race and, although I am just a single human being—indeed, even a shabby thief—arrogantly pretended to be the whole human race?⁵⁸

At first, the above statement may seem quite odd. Why does Climacus characterize the poet as a robber? The answer is that, the poet, for Climacus, stands as a witness of the occurrence of the descent of the god into History. The poet is reporting a poem that he did not write; he is a poet in virtue of the fact that he is exposing an event that has unfolded poetically. Climacus refers to the occurrence as a wonder: "Is not the whole thing a wondrous, does not this word come to my lips as a felicitously foreshadowing word, for do we not, as I in fact said and you yourself involuntary say, stand here before *the wonder*."⁵⁹

Climacus on Hegel's View of Socrates

Climacus claims vehemently that the Socratic teaching relation is an ideal, which is not prevalent in his time. The absence of the Socratic teaching is due to the fact that "our age, after all, has the positive and is a connoisseur of it, whereas Socrates lacked the positive."⁶⁰ However, Climacus does not elaborate further upon what he means by the positive. He simply goes on to provide more details about the nature of the Socratic relation, which suggests a pejorative definition of the positive. Climacus defines the positive through what it is not. For Climacus:

> Between one human being and another, this is the highest: the pupil is the occasion for the teacher to understand himself; the teacher is the occasion for the pupil to understand himself; in death the teacher leaves no claim upon the pupil's soul, no more than the pupil can claim that the teacher owes him something.⁶¹

Despite this indirect discussion, Climacus's use of the positive requires further investigation, since it is a direct allusion to his contemporaries. In the first chapter, Climacus converses mainly with the Hellenic tradition through the assessment of recollection. It seems that in this chapter, Climacus is critiquing the teaching approach of his contemporaries. To understand Climacus's position, we need to inquire further about who and what he is referring to through the claim that his age is a 'connoisseur' of the positive.

If we follow Hong's comment, Climacus is alluding to either Hegel or Schelling. His statement about Socrates's lack of the positive is a reference to Hegel's discussion of Socrates in his *History of Philosophy*. "Presumably a reference to Hegel and Hegelians, perhaps also to Schelling."[62] Let us then take up Hong's suggestion and consider Hegel's characterization of Socrates. Indeed, Hong is correct to assume that Climacus is referring to Hegel's view of Socrates, which Kierkegaard develops in an early work. Climacus's claim that Socrates lacks the positive is fundamental to understand his view of the Socratic teaching as the ideal relationship. Climacus's assertion needs to be further developed in order to elucidate his interpretation of Socrates and to make explicit his criticism of Hegel's account of Socrates.

The earliest interpretation of Socrates in Kierkegaard's corpus is presented in the first part of his dissertation: *The Concept of Irony* (1841). In this work, Kierkegaard starts with an assessment of the accounts of Socrates life from Xenophon, Plato, and Aristophanes. After delineating each account, Kierkegaard then focuses on Hegel's view of Socrates, in his *History of Philosophy*. For Kierkegaard, Hegel considers Socrates as the original incarnation of subjectivity in the World Spirit. Socrates's uniqueness consists in his awareness of the relationship of the individual's consciousness to the established norms of the state. This awareness constitutes the rise of subjectivity through the acknowledgement of the ability to choose. "Thus with Socrates the deciding spirit is transformed into the subjective consciousness of man, since the power of deciding originates with himself; and the first question now is, how this subjectivity appears in Socrates himself."[63] For Hegel, the awareness of the ability to choose is distinct from conscience because the latter is based upon the mere internalization of the ruling norms of the state. The manifestation of conscience is the individual's deliberation upon the laws of the state which she regards as necessary and irreplaceable. That's why Hegel states regarding Socrates's *daimon* that:

> The characteristic form in which this subjectivity—this implicit and deciding certainty—appears in Socrates, has still to be mentioned. That is since everyone here has this personal mind which appears to him to be his mind, we see how in connection with this, we have what is known under the name of the Genius (δαιμόνιον) of Socrates...But in this Genius of Socrates—notorious as a much discussed *bizarrerie* of his imagination—we are neither to imagine the existence of protective spirit, angel, and such-like, nor even of conscience. "

Kierkegaard thinks that Hegel regards Socrates to be acting in accordance with his genius and not following his conscience because he extricates his consciousness from the objective which is the set of established laws of the state. As this claim shows: "For conscience is the idea of universal individuality, of the mind certain of itself, which is at the same time universal truth."[65] According to Hegel, Socrates's genius is the expression of his subjective consciousness independently of the norms of the state. Socrates's uniqueness is the fact that he is able to reflect upon the mere ability for self-individualization. "But that his pure consciousness stood above both, sides is clearly what I have expressed by saying that he had the idea of the good as the infinite negativity."[66]

For Kierkegaard, Hegel's characterization of Socrates, as the founder of morality is grounded precisely in the above account. Socrates's consciousness is the illustration of the consciousness, which is able to contemplate *being-in-and-for-itself*. Socrates was able to reflect upon the form of consciousness, as the negative, and its object, which is the positive. That is why Hegel claims that: "In this consciousness he elevated morality into perception, but this action is just the bringing to consciousness of the fact that it is the power of the notion which sublates the determinate existence and the immediate value of moral laws and the sacredness of their implicitude."[67] Kierkegaard relies on Hegel's claim to conclude that: "Thus Socrates has arrived at being-in-and-for itself as the being-in-and-for itself for thought. This is the one element; the other is that this good, this universal, must be recognized by me."[68]

Socrates is the bearer of the negative, according to Hegel, through the ability of his consciousness to adopt an aloof attitude toward the social norms of the state. Laws and traditions represent the objective aspect of ethics, which is distinct from morality, as the individual's conscious reflection upon the norms that are prevalent in the state. Kierkegaard observes that: "He [Hegel] distinguishes between *morality* and *ethics*. But ethics is in part unreflected ethics such as Ancient Greek ethics, and in part a higher determination of it such as manifests itself again after having recollected itself in morality."[69] The moral agent enjoys negative freedom because her consciousness is not passively determined by the norms of the state that represent the positive. "Here the moral individual is the negatively free individual. He is free because he is not bound by another, but he is negatively free precisely because he is not limited in another."[70]

Kierkegaard seems to think that Hegel's account of Socrates, as the founder of morality, has both, a beneficial and detrimental outcome. The detrimental result is that Socrates's introduction of subjective consciousness at this stage of the

World Spirit is disruptive for the harmony of the Greek *Polis*. "The individual should no longer act out of fear of the law but with a conscious knowledge of why he acted. But this, as we shall see, is a negative definition, negative toward the established order as well as negative toward the deeper positivity, which, as speculative, conditions negatively."[71] On the other hand, the beneficial aspect of this discovery, which Hegel fails to acknowledge, consists in the fact that it liberates the individual from the blind rule of the state. "Hegel did not really disapprove of Socrates's Irony, because he failed to grasp its full importance; he represented it as a weak concept and reduced it to a simple 'moment', a stage in dialectics, without seeing its infinite and absolute negativity."[72]

It is through the infinite and absolute negativity that the individual can conceive of herself as a free subjectivity. Hegel's view of Socratic Irony is consistent with his disapproval of the freedom of the particular from the universal. However, this aspect is the core of the Socratic teaching method, which Climacus posits as the basis of his discussion of Socratic teaching in the *Philosophical Fragments* because of the priority that it grants to subjective relationship over universal ones. The privilege of consciousness to remain attached or distant from the objective state of affairs represents Irony; the ironic attitude is the ability of consciousness to adopt a contemplative stance toward the positive. The fact that Socrates assumes an ironic attitude toward the positive is the linchpin of Socratic teaching, which is suitable to elevate the learner existentially.

Paradox: The Passion of Thought

In the chapter, *The Absolute Paradox*, Climacus takes up the impact of the role of the god as the servant upon the learner's understanding. To ease his way in the discussion of the paradox, Climacus cites the paradoxical position of Socrates, who despite his impressive grasp of the human condition did not deem himself sophisticated enough to engage in the contemplation of metaphysical matters. Hence, the paradox is a necessary counterpart of the thinking process to which even Socrates was not an exception. Climacus states: "But one must not think ill of the paradox, for the paradox is the passion of thought, and the thinker without the paradox is like the lover without passion: a mediocre fellow."[73] The passion is the unavoidable constituent of thought, which could be detrimental to thought: "But the ultimate potentiation of every passion is always to will its own downfall. This, then, is the ultimate paradox of thought: to want to discover something that thought itself cannot think."[74] The development of the antithetical relation between thought and the absolute passion is the theme of the third chapter.

Climacus sets up another proposition that is fundamental to the infrastructure of the chapter. As a working hypothesis, he presupposes the *telos* of all Ancient philosophical enterprises in the claim that: "But in order to get started, let us state a bold proposition: let us assume that we know what a human being is. In this we do indeed have the criterion of truth, which all Greek Philosophy *sought,* or *doubted,* or *postulated,* or *brought to fruition.*"[75] This proposition is provisional because a few passages later, Climacus states that the paradox of the understanding subverts the learner's conviction about her self-knowledge: "so also that intimated paradox of the understanding reacts upon a person and upon his self-knowledge in such a way that he who believed that he knew himself now no longer is sure whether he perhaps is a more curiously complex animal than Typhon or whether he has in his being a gentler and diviner part"[76] The paradox, as the passion of thought, threatens the learner's certainty about self-knowledge; it sets the basis for the learner to reconsider the basis of self-knowledge. The inner turmoil that the learner experiences is not occasioned by a familiar phenomenon. Thus, for Climacus, the baffling of the understanding is the consequence of its encounter with an unusual entity. Climacus summarizes this event in the following: "But what is this unknown against which the understanding in its paradoxical passion collides and which even disturbs man and his self-knowledge? It is the unknown. But it is not a human being, insofar as he knows man, or anything else that he knows. Therefore let us call this unknown *the god.*"[77] Climacus emphasizes the semantic nature of the qualification to avoid an ontological misunderstanding. The god *is* not the unknown. For the understanding, it only has semantic purpose because it does not denote divinity, but represents only a referent.

Besides, it is important to bear in mind that Climacus is here proceeding under the assumed position of the learner. Seen from the standpoint of the understanding, the unknown is a demarcating concept for what the understanding has not yet fully grasped. "It is only a name we give to it. It hardly occurs to the understanding to want to demonstrate that this unknown (the god) exists. If, namely, the god does not exist, then of course it is impossible to demonstrate it."[78] Thus, Climacus posits the god through a nominalist position; it is merely a name that does not yet have a specific and definite ontological status for the understanding. However, the understanding faces a dilemma when contemplating the unknown. To start a demonstration of the god is self-defeating because one cannot show the existence of a non-existent. Any demonstration automatically asserts the existence of what is to be proven.

> But if he does exist, then it is foolishness to want to demonstrate it, since I, in the very moment the demonstration commences, would presuppose it not as doubtful—which a presupposition cannot be, inasmuch as it is a presupposition—but as decided, because otherwise I would not begin, easily perceiving that the whole thing would be impossible if he did not exist."

For Climacus, the alternative approach would be to attempt to connect the concept of the unknown with that of the god. But this strategy fails because it is merely the expansion of the concept of the unknown.

> If, however, I interpret the expression 'to demonstrate the existence of the god' to mean that I want to demonstrate that the unknown, which exists, is the god, then I do not express myself very felicitously, for then I demonstrate nothing, least of all an existence, but I develop the definition of a concept.⁸⁰

This process still fails to grasp the god for what it is essentially; it is merely an indirect apprehension of the god by means of another concept. Climacus's aim is to show the elusive nature of the god and to establish the central conclusion that is going to guide the exposition. Reasoning has to start from the existent and that one may not reason toward an existent. "Therefore, whether I am moving in the world of sensate palpability or in the world of thought, I never reason in conclusion to existence, but I reason in conclusion from existence. For example, I do not demonstrate that a stone exists but that something which exists is a stone."[81] Climacus asserts clearly the priority of the existent before it is conceptualized as a stone.

Climacus uses the example of the relation between Napoleon and his deeds to show that the association between Napoleon's existence and his actions is arbitrary because it is a finite relation. The existence of Napoleon, as an individual, cannot be inferred from his achievements; only the existence of a great general may be posited. "If I ignore this, I can never demonstrate (purely ideally) that such works are the works of a great general etc."[82] Thus, inferring from individual and finite accomplishments can only yield the universal and not the particular. Climacus contrasts this individual relation with that of the divine, because the god's existence is derivable from his achievements. This is feasible in virtue of the absolute relation between the god and his accomplishments. "However, between the god and his works there is an absolute relation. God is not a name but a concept, and perhaps because of that his *essentia invovit existentiam* [essence involves existence]."[83] With this claim, Climacus asserts the difference between the finite domain and that of the god. God is a concept because it is sufficient in itself; his existence and essence are not two distinct moments.

To support his view of the relation between the god and his manifestations, Climacus assesses Spinoza's account of God. According to Climacus, the fundamental premise, from which Spinoza proceeds, is the association of *being* with *perfection*; for Spinoza, more being necessarily entails more perfection. The isomorphic relation between perfection and being implies a correlation between ontology and divinity; the divine is perfect because it enjoys the most being. Climacus sums up his interpretation of Spinoza's view in the following: "He [Spinoza] explains *perfectio* by *realitas, esse* [perfection...reality, being]. Consequently, the more perfect the thing is, the more it *is;* but its perfection is that it has more *esse* in itself, which means that the more it is, the more it is.—So much for the tautology."[84] The fundamental flaw of Spinoza's view, according to Climacus, is that he fails to differentiate between ideality and actuality. The ideal and the real are different because the latter has more being, but they are not intrinsically different. Spinoza conflates *esse* with *realitas* despite their different natures. "But to go on, what is lacking here is a distinction between factual being and ideal being."[85] Climacus distinguishes his position from Spinoza's view by positing an absolute relation between God and his deeds. Hence, in doing so, Climacus manages to preserve the distinction between reality and ideality. The ideality of God, as the concept, has an absolute association with the factual God, the works of God. The particularity of God's works, thus, yields the genus God.

Climacus, then, sets out to account for what may be considered as the god's works. According to his standpoint, there are two ways to grasp the god's deeds. The first one is through immediacy. It is to regard as the god's works, the totality of the concrete objects of existence as perception presents them to us. The problem with immediacy, however, is that it cannot account for the harmony between the horrors of earthly existence and divine omnipotence. "The works from which I want to demonstrate his existence do not immediately and directly exist, not at all...Do we not encounter the most terrible spiritual trials here, and is it ever possible to be finished with all these trials?"[86] This option fails because of the lack of continuous goodness and harmony in the domain of perceptual existence. Perceptual existence can only offer a fragmented picture of the accomplishments of the god. "But I still do not demonstrate God's existence from such an order of things, and even if I began, I would never finish and also would be obliged continually to live *in suspenso* lest something so terrible happen that my fragment of demonstration would be ruined."[87]

The trials that Climacus mentions represent the presence of evil in social experience, which cannot be reconciled with divine goodness. The second way is ideality, which considers the works of the god from an ideal perspective and overlooks the immediate. In the ideal outlook on the works of the god, one regards the facts of reality, as they ought to be. It is in agreement with the form of traditional logic which relates to reality ideally. However, the limit of ideality, for Climacus, consists in the fact that it merely ascribes to the god an existence in the conceptual domain. "From the works regarded ideally—that is, as they do not appear directly and immediately. But then I do not demonstrate it from the works, after all, but only develop the ideality I have presupposed;"[88] As one commentator observes: "Kierkegaard is thinking primarily of something like traditional logic and such logical laws as the principle of non-contradiction or the law of the excluded middle, understood as principles for evaluating propositions but not as providing information about the contents of the world."[89]

For Climacus, the genuine manifestation of the god's works is possible only if it is not brought about by any rational demonstration. Both, ideality and immediacy depend upon either sensory or conceptual interpretation. The god's works can arise only independently of the subsumption of both, ideality and immediacy, which already posit interpretation and expectation as discursive processes. "So also with the demonstration—so long as I am holding on to the demonstration (that is continue to be one who is demonstrating), the existence does not emerge, if for no other reason than that I am in the process of demonstrating it, but when I let go of the demonstration, the existence is there."[90] It is noteworthy that Climacus is drawing an implicit contrast between 'emerge' and 'demonstrating'. The former suggests the free emanation of the works of the god, whereas the latter suggests the coercive and external determinations of the rational processes. Although the emergence of the works of God may suggest the passivity of the sensory and rational faculties, Climacus states that it is the active determination of the individual. "Yet this letting go, even that is surely something; it is after all, *meine Zuthat* [my contribution]."[91] The means through which it comes about is a cessation of the discursive process of rationality. Climacus characterizes this event by a theme, which is essential to Kierkegaardian terminologies. The *leap* represents the alternative between ideality and immediacy, which makes the emergence of the works of the god possible. "Does it not have to be taken into account, this diminutive moment, however brief it is—it does not have to be long, because it is a *leap*."[92] The *leap* is a sudden interruption of the conceptualization process of rationality. Its suddenness lies in its brevity, which opens up a different type of experience beyond the immediate and the ideal.

The introduction of the *leap* elucidates Climacus's intention at the beginning of the chapter by introducing the premise regarding the knowledge of human nature. The refutation of the premise has indeed yielded a new discovery for thought. The *leap* is paradoxical because it represents both, the expansion of thought and the indication of its insufficiency. By making a new experiential horizon available to the individual, it points out the insufficiency of the two usual modes of experience, immediacy and ideality, and provides a third possibility for experience. The perplexity that accompanies the rise of the paradox of the understanding is essential to the preparation for the acquisition of this new possibility. Thus, Climacus indirectly asserts the suspension of the rational faculty as the source of the confusion, which arises as a necessity for the occurrence of the *leap*. Climacus's formulation of the leap as the occasion for the emergence of the works of the god establishes the subjective certainty of the concept of God. The existence of the god depends on the subjective appropriation by the self.

For Climacus, the understanding is unable to avoid the confusion of the paradox. The unknown represents a mandatory negative concept, whose existence even when it is denied by the understanding reinforces their relationship. This relationship is concomitant to the fact that the denial of the understanding presupposes the existence of what is being denied. That's why Climacus states that the understanding is continually mired in the paradox. "The understanding does not go beyond this; yet in its paradoxicality the understanding cannot stop reaching it and being engaged with it, because wanting to express its relation to it by saying that this unknown does not exist will not do, since just saying that involves a relation."[93] Hence, Climacus considers the unknown as the tantalizing concept of the understanding. The understanding may only contemplate it as the unreachable; it cannot conceptualize and transcend the unknown in the face of which it comes to despair. Climacus introduces the notion of the *unknown* to express the divine from the standpoint of the understanding. It is the god who stands as the limit of the rational faculty.

> But what, then, is this unknown, for does not its being the god merely signify to us that it is the unknown? To declare that it is the unknown because we cannot know it, and that even if we could know it we could not express it, does not satisfy the passion, although it has correctly perceived the unknown as frontier. But a frontier is expressly the passion's torment, even though it is also an incentive. And yet it can go no further, whether it risks a sortie through *via negationis* [the way through negation] or *via eminentiae* [the way of idealization].[94]

Several important implications follow from Climacus's statement. The first one is that Climacus assumes the inadequacy of language to account for the existence of the god, by saying that even if the understanding could grasp the unknown it would not be able to express it. Thus the unknown lies beyond the grasp of both, the understanding and language. The second one is Climacus's allusion to the Thomist notion of God as the limiting concept of the understanding, and that conceiving divinity requires the negation of the intellect, which occurs by attributing to the divine the qualities that it lacks. Climacus here presupposes the Thomist notion of the *via negationis*.

Climacus then delves into the understanding's conception of the unknown. The main question that Climacus is attempting to address is: How does the understanding conceive of this limiting notion? Since the notion of the unknown stands as a negative concept, which the understanding must attempt to grasp, Climacus sheds some light by emphasizing the grasp of the unknown as the different. The understanding's inability to contemplate the unknown directly is summed up in Climacus's definition of the different. "What, then, is the unknown? It is the frontier that is continually arrived at, and therefore when the category of motion is replaced by the category of rest it is the different, the absolutely different."[95] The fact that Climacus ascribes absoluteness to the unknown as the different seems to be in order to anticipate the following objection: Upon what ground can the understanding attribute existence to what lies beyond its limit? This plausible objection is important because there are two ways to think of the unknown as a limiting concept. It might be thought of as a limit beyond which nothing lies. In this case, the understanding acknowledges its limitation, which opens up a new horizon that remains beyond its grasp. The second way to think of the unknown as limiting is, as that which announces an absolutely foreign horizon to the grasp of the understanding, which is impregnable to thought. Climacus is using the absolutely different in the second way, as the absolutely other. This fact can be inferred by reflecting on the following statement:

> But it is the absolutely different in which there is no distinguishing mark. Defined as the absolutely different, it seems to be at the point of being disclosed, but not so, because the understanding cannot even think the absolutely different; it cannot absolutely negate itself but uses itself for that purpose and consequently thinks the difference in itself, which it thinks by itself.[96]

The claim that the absolutely different is that *in which* there is no distinguishing mark asserts the existence of the absolutely different without any difference in itself. How can that be? The answer to this question is that Climacus is assuming the finite side of the understanding to define the absolutely different. The absolutely different has no distinguishing mark because it is viewed from the perspective of the understanding; to the understanding the absolutely different is the orgiastic. It is upon this fact that we may conclude that Climacus is defining the unknown as a limit according to the second approach. In addition, the second clause of the above statement is enlightening. What does Climacus mean by stating that 'defined as the absolutely different, it seems to be at the point of being disclosed'? Climacus seems to be aware that the linguistic definition of the unknown may suggest that it is accessible to the understanding since it can be formulated linguistically. To avoid such misinterpretation, he reinforces that 'the understanding cannot even think the absolutely different'. Thus the only option of the understanding is to contemplate the unknown as the limit, as the 'in-itself'. This last option is reminding of the Kantian relation of the categories and the *noumena*. The manifestation of the god to the understanding is comparable to those of the appearances of the in-itself to the understanding in Kant's Philosophy. Climacus reaches the conclusion that the understanding may only attempt to overcome its impotence by positing the absolutely different as the fantastic. "The unknown is then in διασπορά [dispersion], and the understanding has an attractive selection from among what is available and what fantasy can think of (the prodigious, the ridiculous, etc.)."[97]

However, for Climacus, only an illusion can result from a fantastic contemplation of the unknown. The illusion consists in generating the god through religious devotion. The god thus emanates as the outcome of faithful devotion to the idea of divinity. "But this difference cannot be grasped securely. Every time this happens, it is basically an arbitrariness, and at the very bottom of devoutness there madly lurks the capricious arbitrariness that knows it itself has produced the god."[98] The problem is that the god is the product of the idea of divinity; it succumbs to Deism. The rejection of this possibility shows Climacus's resistance to a subjectivist basis to the existence of the god. The existence of the god is to be reached through the subjective and existential appropriation of his accomplishments.

The second possibility that Climacus refutes is the identical relation that may result from the difference between the understanding and the unknown. According to Climacus, the understanding's impotence to grasp the absolutely different may lead it to conflate it with its own nature. In this occurrence, the understanding no longer regards the unknown as the other, but appropriates it by elevating itself as absolute. "If the difference cannot be grasped securely because there is no distinguishing mark, then, as with all such dialectical opposites, so it is with the difference and likeness—they are identical. Adhering to the understanding, the difference has so confused the understanding that it does not know itself and quite consistently confuses itself with the difference."[99] In this claim, Climacus rules out the possibility of dialectical mediation as a means to overcome the difference between the understanding and the god. Climacus seems to be avoiding the Fichtean reduction of the object of the *I* to the essence of the *I* as the frame for the relation; the god and the understanding are not suitable for the *I-I* relationship in Fichte's account of the infinite subject. The difference of the god is absolute and dumbfounds the understanding in resisting the possibility of synthesis.

Climacus removes the god from the epistemological purview of the understanding by characterizing the god as the deceiver of the understanding. The deceptive relation of the understanding with the unknown thus makes it necessary to set up a different relation between the individual and the unknown. In Climacus's words:

> Well, I cannot know it, for in that case I would have to know the god and the difference, and I do not know the difference, inasmuch as the understanding has made it like unto that from which it differs. Thus the god has become the most terrible deceiver through the understanding's deception of itself. The understanding has the god as close as possible and yet just as far way.[100]

Hence, Climacus is suggesting that the understanding must cease its rational functions to relate to the unknown. Climacus personifies his reader's suggestion to adopt the following alternative: " 'I would have to lock everything out of my consciousness in order to think of it.' That is exactly what you have to do, but then is it justifiable to want to keep all the presuppositions *you* have in your consciousness and still presume to think about your consciousness without any presuppositions?"[101] Climacus's objection to the alternative, indeed, shows that he is aware of its inherent absurdity. The absurdity consists in the fact that consciousness intrinsically performs rational functions. The *form* of consciousness may not operate without specific set of presuppositions. Thus Climacus is indirectly suggesting that the experience of the unknown is only possible unless it baffles consciousness.

That Climacus wishes to forsake the discursive side of consciousness in the consideration of the unknown becomes explicit when he posits the intervention of the god as the different to become manifest. It is noteworthy that although Climacus employs the verb *to know*, it has been neutralized from its epistemological relation with consciousness. *To know* expresses the paradox, according to which the experience of the unknown requires the cessation of knowing as a rational process. Climacus elaborates that in the following: "At this point we seem to stand at a paradox. Just to come to know that the god is the different, man needs the god and then comes to know that the god is the absolutely different."[102] Thus the nature of the god is dual; it is both, the different and the condition to know the different. It is in virtue of its dual function that the god is the absolutely different.

The disparity between the godly and human nature originates in the inadequacy, which is intrinsic to humanity. "What, then, is the difference? Indeed, what else but sin, since the difference, the absolute difference, must have been caused by the individual himself."[103] Thus, for Climacus, the negative impact of *sin* upon human nature is twofold. It is the cause of the insufficiency of the understanding to grasp the unknown. Also, it permeates the other aspect of individuality by making it unworthy of the divine. Thus, *sin* is responsible for both, a rational impediment and the unworthiness of humanity before the divine.

The individual then grasps the absolutely different in acknowledging her sinful state. The individual's realization that *sin* is the intrinsic imperfection that pervades human nature sheds light upon Climacus's dismissal of the understanding as the rational faculty to apprehend the divine. The god, as absolute difference, becomes manifest to the self through the consciousness of sin, which is elusive to rational apprehension. Climacus expresses the elusiveness of sin by using Socrates, whose rational approach was unable to conceive of *sin*. "What did he lack then? The consciousness of sin, which he could no more teach to any other person than any other person could teach it to him. Only the god could teach it—if he wanted to be teacher."[104] Climacus posits the teacher as the one who provides the individual the possibility to acquire the consciousness of sin. The chapter ends with emphasis on the difference between the Hellenic tradition and the Christian experience.

Climacus is consistently striving to transcend Socrates and to assert the necessity of the Christian experience. He emphasizes the shortcoming of Socrates in order to illustrate the necessity for the Christian consciousness of sin. Although this fact might suggest that Climacus intends to demonstrate the insufficiency of the Hellenic tradition, however, it determines the necessity of the Christian moment. The Christian moment is meant to complement the Hellenic approach that is embodied in Socrates. Hence, Climacus regards the Hellenic tradition and the Christian experience as two indispensable moments in the acquisition of the condition from the god. Climacus wishes to establish continuity between Socrates and Christ; Christ picks up at the juncture where Socratic guidance falls short. For Climacus, it seems that the coming of Christ, as the savior and reconciler, was to carry out the completion of Socratic guidance. Moreover, the continuity between Socrates and Christ is consistent with History as the temporal basis through which the self can reach eternal happiness.

Kantian Judgment and the Works of God

One of the themes of this chapter which needs further consideration is Climacus's thesis that: *One cannot reason to existence and that the existent is prior conceptualization.* Climacus illustrates his conclusion with the example of the stone, which as an existent precedes the concept of 'stoneness'. Climacus's conclusion needs further analysis in order to bring out the implicit reference of his claim. Climacus elaborates the above conclusion in a draft, he states:

> I never reason in conclusion to existence (for in that case I would be mad to want to reason in conclusion to what I know), but I reason in conclusion from existence and am so accommodating to popular opinion as to call it a demonstrative argument. Thus the connection is somewhat different from what Kant meant—that existence is an *accesorium*[addition]—although therein he undeniably has an advantage over Hegel in that he does not confuse.[105]

Climacus makes it explicit that he is alluding to Kant's position that existence is not a predicate. Existence is the ontological basis in virtue of which the attribution of a predicate is made possible. Climacus's statement offers sufficient evidence to believe that he must have been familiar with Kant's discussion of this fact in the *Critique of Pure Reason.* Kant argues that to assert existence, as a predicate, which represents an addendum to what is already evident is tautologous. To attribute existence to a 'this' or 'that' does not enrich what is being defined, but merely reiterates that it is. Kant states:

> My answer is as follows. There is already a contradiction in introducing the concept of existence—no matter under what title it may be disguised—into the concept of a thing which we profess to be thinking solely in reference to its possibility. If that be allowed as legitimate, a seeming victory has been won; but in actual fact nothing at all is said: the assertion is a mere tautology.[106]

According to Kant, claiming that existence is part of the concept of a 'this' or 'that' does not reveal any novelty about that which is being defined. For Kant existence is already captured in the very copula *'is'* which makes the act of judgment feasible. " *'Being'* is obviously not a real predicate; that is, it is not a concept of something which could be added to the concept of a thing. It is merely the positing of a thing, or of certain determinations, as existing in themselves. Logically it is merely the copula of a judgment."¹⁰⁷ Kant sets up existence as the basis of judgment; the association of the subject and a predicate is possible upon the confirmation of the subject via the copula 'is'.

Climacus relies on Kant's account of existence to show that it is tenable only in the context of finite judgments. He uses the example of Napoleon, whose very existence already presupposes the works of Napoleon; to utter the name of Napoleon is concurrent with citing the sum of his achievements. Climacus thinks that: "If one wanted to demonstrate Napoleon's existence from Napoleon's works, would it not be most curious, since his existence certainly explains the works but the works do not demonstrate *his* existence unless I have already in advance interpreted the word 'his' in such a way as to have assumed that he exists."¹⁰⁸ However, Climacus's accentuation on the fact that Napoleon's existence already implies his achievements is a one way assertion that may not be reversed. The deeds of Napoleon do not contain the existence of the individual Napoleon, but refer to those of a general. "If I ignore this, I can never demonstrate from the works that they are Napoleon's but demonstrate (purely ideally) that such works are the works of a great general."¹⁰⁹

For Climacus, the act of judgment does not hold in the case of the god's works. This is why he characterizes the god as a concept whose essence and existence are one and the same. The existence of the god is intrinsically linked with his works; and the works of the god amount to the essence of the god. "However, between the god and his works there is an absolute relation. God is not a name but a concept, and perhaps because of that his *essentia involvit existentiam* [essence involves existence]."¹¹⁰ Climacus's intention, through the reference to Kant's account of existence, is to show that Kantian judgment cannot accommodate the relation between the existence of the god and his works, which it would have to regard as predicates.

Yet the second part of Climacus's statement in the draft needs assessment, as well, mainly that Kant's account of existence is privileged over that of Hegel's. Climacus's contention becomes clear under the consideration of Hegel's discussion of the existence of finite entities and God in the chapter on being in the *Science of Logic*. After arguing in favor of the intrinsic unity of pure being and nothing in abstraction, Hegel offers his reflection upon Kant's account of existence that is developed above. Using Kant's famous example of the concept of the hundred dollars, Hegel provides his position upon the existence of finite entities and that of God. According to Hegel, the concept of the hundred dollars is different from one hundred real dollars because the former is considered independently from other entity. It is a concept because it has not been determined in relation to other finite entities; the concept is that which is in a domain by itself. "Because this difference is so obvious with the hundred dollars, therefore the concept, that is, the specific nature of the content as an empty possibility, and being, are different from each other"[111] For Hegel, the concept and its object are distinct only because the former has not yet passed into the latter to be differentiated from other entities. Hegel maintains that God is no exception to this relation. Given that the being of the hundred dollars cannot be inferred from its concept, it is equally absurd to claim to derive the existence of God from the concept, as the ontological proof does. "*therefore* the Notion of God too is different from his being, and just as little as I can extract from the possibility of the hundred dollars their actuality, just as little can I extract from the Notion of God his existence; but the ontological proof is supposed to consist of this extraction of the existence of God from his Notion."[112] Hence, Hegel discards the traditional distinction between the nature of God and that of finite entities, which is based upon the view that the former's essence and existence can be mutually inferred. Hegel concludes his criticism of the ontological proof by asserting that the underlying incentive of the ontological proof is to eliminate any continuity between the finite domain and that of God: "The genuine criticism of the categories and of reason is just this: to make intellect aware of this difference and to prevent it from applying to God the determinations and relationships of the finite."[113]

Climacus's resistance to Hegel's account derives from his attempt to maintain the separation between the finite and God. Hegel's account is in direct opposition to Climacus's claim about the inseparability of God's existence and his works, which is based upon the ontological argument. If the concept of God is indeed God that has not been differentiated from other entities and is 'the empty possibility' of God in actuality, then Climacus's assertion that the concept of God and the works of God can be mutually inferred fail. Although, Climacus is criticizing both, Kant and Hegel in his discussion of existence, it is in agreement with his position to privilege the Kantian account because it is closer to his own characterization than that of Hegel.

Offense as Suffering

Climacus goes on to suggest two possible relations between the understanding and the paradox. The first relation yields a positive outcome. As the agreement between the understanding and the paradox, the first relation is a 'happy encounter' of the two parties. In this relation, the understanding accepts the absolutely different, as another, which does not conform to its usual process of conceptualization. The faculty of the understanding adopts a positive attitude toward the inherent difference of the paradox. The understanding is brought to realize the autonomy of the paradox in spite of its non-cognitive character. On the other hand, the second relation represents the refutation of the dissimilarity of the absolutely different by the understanding. The understanding refuses to accommodate the essential difference of the paradox. As the opposite of the former relation, the disagreement between the understanding and the paradox results in suffering. For Climacus, the negative relation of the paradox and the understanding constitutes the *offense*. "If the encounter is not in mutual understanding, then the relation is unhappy, and the understanding's unhappy love, if I dare call it that ... we could more specifically term *offense*."[114] The offense of the understanding toward the paradox is expressed in the subjective experience of turmoil. The tumultuous experience of the understanding derives from its resistance to the paradox. Climacus states that: "At its deepest level, all offense is a suffering."[115] However, the distressful experience of the understanding is not apparent, for Climacus, because it undergoes suffering in a passive manner.

Climacus elaborates on the suffering of the *offense* in a footnote, in which he draws attention to the fact that the nature of suffering as an affect is often overlooked. "Our language correctly terms an uncontrolled emotional state [*Affekt*] a *suffering* of the mind [*Sinds lidelse*], although when using the word 'affect' we usually think of the convulsive boldness that astounds us, and because of that we forget that it is a suffering. For example, arrogance, defiance, etc."[116] Climacus is here elaborating the experience of subjective suffering. Suffering is here different from its popular meaning; it is not an immediate and observable state of the individual. Rather, Climacus's definition of suffering as an 'affect' is meant to draw out the passive nature of the understanding's experience of the *offense*. The passive aspect of the *offense* is important because of its implicit reference to despair.

According to Climacus, the difference between the passive suffering of the offense and active suffering consists in the permanence of the former. The passive suffering of the offense manifests itself in its uniformity, which makes it continuous. On the other hand, active offense endures in virtue of its impotence. Active offence persists because it is unable to extricate itself from the paradox. Climacus explains the difference between passive and active *offense* in the following claim:

> We can, however, very well distinguish between suffering offense and active offense, yet without forgetting that suffering offense is always active to the extent that it cannot altogether allow itself to be annihilated (for offense is always an act, not an event), and active offense is always weak enough to be incapable of tearing

itself loose from the cross to which it is nailed or to pull out the arrow with which it is wounded."[117]

Indeed, the ambiguity of Climacus's account of the difference between active and passive suffering is not accidental. At first, the distinction may seem insignificant since there is no direct contrast between the two accounts. Moreover, Climacus complicates the second definition by using a metaphor. The motive of his strategy becomes evident in the following paragraph when he claims that it is precisely because of its nature that the passive suffering of the *offense* is elusive to the understanding. Thus, the confusing nature of Climacus's account of the difference was meant to illustrate the inability of the understanding to grasp the *offense*. "But precisely because offense is a suffering in this manner, the discovery, if it may be put this way, does not belong to the understanding but to the paradox, for just as truth is *index sui et falsi* [the criterion of itself and of the false], so also is the paradox"[118] Suffering is not graspable by the understanding because it belongs to the relation of the offense and the paradox; it is in essence a subjective experience.

Moreover, the impotence of the understanding prevents it from being conscious of its state of offense. Climacus's account points out that the understanding is so enmeshed in the experience of turmoil that it is unfit to assess the state in which it is. Climacus is here viewing the understanding from the perspective of the paradox. The paradox is both, the initiator and the standard of the offense. "So the offense is not the origination of the understanding—far from it, for then the understanding must also have been able to originate with the paradox. No the offense *comes into existence* with the paradox; if it *comes into existence*, here again we have the moment around which everything indeed revolves."[119] The understanding's misidentification of this new experience as its own creation is an *acoustical* illusion; the understanding mistakes the voice of the paradox for its own. "Thus, although the offense, however it expresses itself, sounds from somewhere else—indeed, from the opposite corner—nevertheless it is the paradox that resounds in it, and this indeed is an acoustical illusion."[120] For Climacus, the understanding is erring when it grapples with the *offense* as an epistemological concept, since it belongs intrinsically to the domain of the paradox. The *offense* belongs within the paradox, as the passion of the understanding. Consequently, the understanding is self-deceiving by dealing with the *offense* as its creation. As the description suggests the *offense* is merely reflected in the understanding, its genuine position is within the paradox.

Climacus is here engaged in delineating the categories that represent the infrastructure of the paradox. These categories are antithetical to the rational domain of the understanding because they belong to the absolutely different. Climacus asserts that the relation of the paradox and the offense is deepened in accordance with the passion of the latter: "The more deeply the expression of offense is couched in passion (acting or suffering), the more manifest is the extent to which the offense is indebted to the paradox."[181] The offense is the expression of the understanding's refusal to comply with the paradox as the absolutely different. Since the existential expression of the paradox consists in the moment, the offense thus expresses the misapprehension of the moment. For Climacus, the offense is the dual expression of both, the existential and epistemological collision of the understanding and the absolutely different. "it is nevertheless important to maintain that all offense is in its essence a misunderstanding of the *moment*, since it is indeed offense at the paradox, and the paradox in turn is the moment."[182] The clash of the understanding and the paradox illustrates a conflict within the self. The rational is in conflict with the subjective and results in existential distress.

Climacus elaborates further on the nature of the moment, which is intensified by the rise of the offense. The actual state of the understanding is made significant by and grants significance to the moment. Climacus accentuates the meaningfulness of the moment because it is that which limits the Hellenic tradition and confirms the necessity of the Christian experience.

> Let us recapitulate. If we do not assume the moment, then we go back to Socrates, and it was precisely from him that we wanted to take leave in order to discover something. If the moment is posited, the paradox is there, for in its most abbreviated the paradox can be called the moment. Through the moment, the learner becomes untruth; the person who knew himself becomes confused about himself and instead of self-knowledge he acquires the consciousness of sin etc.[183]

Climacus is emphatic on the moment because it represents the separation of the Socratic and Christian experiences; it is a necessary rupture along the temporal development which disrupts History to prepare the stage for eternal happiness. In the *Appendix*, Climacus discusses the impact of the encounter of the understanding and the paradox by assuming the attitude of each. The understanding and the paradox are the apex of the Greek and the Christian traditions. Climacus is reflecting on the Christian experience—the paradox—from the standpoint of the Greek, which is for him the embodiment of the understanding.

Climacus describes the inner division that arises from the occurrence of the offense by illustrating the understanding's perception of the paradox and that of the paradox toward the understanding. From the perspective of the understanding, the rise of the paradox is an irrational event, which it deems to be absurd. For

Climacus, the offense lies precisely in this disparaging perception of the paradox by the understanding. On the other hand, the paradox regards the understanding as inadequate because it is unfit to grasp the moment of subjective truth. Climacus's account is in the following: "The expression of offense is that the moment is foolishness, the paradox is foolishness—which is the paradox's claim that the understanding is the absurd but which now resounds as an echo from the offense."[124] The inner conflict between the understanding and the paradox is experienced as passive suffering. The subjective experience of turmoil is the outcome of suffering the offense that Climacus described previously.

Thus the offense is indeed a relational notion that Climacus introduces to illustrate the paradox's attitude toward the understanding and vice-versa. One of the implications of Climacus's approach is that he conceives of the self as a duality: the understanding represents the rational, and the paradox kindles subjectivity. These two aspects relate through mutual refutation that results in suffering as their existential pathos. The offense results in suffering because it encapsulates the inner conflict and refutation, which results from the collision of the understanding and the paradox.

The Historical Origin of the Eternal

Chapter four is pivotal to grasp Climacus's account of the relation between History and eternal happiness. Climacus resumes the discussion of the servant, as the provider of the condition to the learner. Climacus proceeds immediately with the description of the servant in order to suggest that the exposition has entered a new phase. The exposition is now going to unfold from the perspective of the Christian period. The previous chapters constituted Climacus's attempt to use the Hellenic tradition while he simultaneously transcends it. The previous *Appendix* is meaningful because it is the textual illustration of the manifestation of the moment, which separates the understanding as the Socratic from the paradox as the Christian experience. Climacus is proceeding in this chapter with the assumption that the transcendence of Socrates—the exemplar of the understanding—has taken place. Climacus shifts his focus to faith as the operative *organon* of the Christian experience. Hence the issue at stake is: How does the learner—after acquiring the condition in time—proceed to achieve eternal happiness? Climacus states the following:

> The contemporary follower, too, obtains a historical point of departure for his eternal consciousness, for he is indeed contemporary with the historical event that does not intend to be a moment of occasion, and this historical event intends to interest him otherwise than merely historically, intends to be the condition for his eternal happiness.[125]

Climacus returns to the relation of the historical and the eternal in this chapter by providing an answer to the above question. After developing the structural concepts of the moment and the paradox, Climacus introduces the *contemporary follower* as the paradigmatic figure through which the appropriation of the historical as an eternal point of departure takes place. Climacus starts by stressing the revolutionary role of the coming of the god as, the teacher. The innovative role of the coming of the god is that it ceases the Socratic relation to establish the possibility of the eternal, which was foreign to the Greeks. Climacus posits the Socratic relation as the highest form of interaction within the historical context. However, the primary shortcoming of the Socratic is that it is limited to the finite. The coming of the god is the necessary counterpart of the Socratic relation in making the eternal available to the historical self. For Climacus, the coming of the god is the crucial occurrence through which the emergence of the paradox, the moment, and the absolutely different have come about. In his words: "Therefore, if the god did not come himself, then everything would remain Socratic, we would not have the moment, and we would fail to obtain the paradox."[126]

Unlike the Socratic approach to teaching, the coming of the god is itself the teaching. The instruction is intrinsic to the coming of the god. It is consistent with its non-historical origin that the coming of the god does not appeal to the rational faculty. It does not need to adopt ignorance as its basis, which can be remedied by recollection. The learner becomes aware of the teaching unless the god has granted him the condition. Thus, to accept the coming of the god as the teaching itself requires that the learner has been conditioned. "The presence of the god in human form—indeed, in the lowly form of a servant—is precisely the teaching, and the god himself must provide the condition; otherwise the learner is unable to understand anything."[127] At this juncture the legitimate questions that arise are: What is the condition? How does the learner receive it? Climacus's previous account of the paradox and the moment in the *Appendix*, was an elaboration of the condition and the way that the learner acquires it. "But that the god provides the condition has already been explicated as the consequence of *the moment,* and we have shown that the moment is the paradox and that without this we come no further but go back to Socrates."[128] The coming of the god is graspable unless the learner has been conditioned to suspend the understanding. The coming of the god gives rise to the paradox which dwells in the passionate domain of faith.

Climacus then proceeds meticulously to show how the will and the imagination, as rational faculties, are unsuitable to relate to the god in order to strengthen his argument that the learner may achieve eternal happiness only through faith. "How, then, does the learner become a believer or a follower? When the understanding is discharged and he receives the condition. When does he receive this? In the moment. This condition, what does he condition? His understanding of the eternal."[129] Moreover, the paradox represents both, the summit and the limit of the understanding. That Climacus views the rise of the paradox as the culmination and the cessation of the Hellenic period is evident in the following claim:

> Any qualification that claims to render the god directly knowable is undoubtedly an approximation milestone, but it registers retrogression rather than progress, movement away from the paradox rather than toward the paradox, back past Socrates and Socratic ignorance.[130]

Climacus's analogy depicts the learner's relation to the paradox in a progressive movement away from the Socratic. The Socratic and the rise of the paradox represent the stages of the learner's ascension toward faith

For Climacus, the learner may overcome the offense by yielding to the first alternative according to which the understanding reconciles itself with the absolute difference of the paradox. Climacus develops this relation further and asserts that the reconciliation of the learner with the paradox creates a new domain mainly that of faith. This new domain opens up through the suspension of the understanding, which allows the paradox to have free reign. According to Climacus's view, the inner dichotomy between faith and understanding is replaced by the prevalence of the paradox in the learner's existence. "It occurs when the understanding and the paradox happily encounter each other in the moment, when the understanding steps aside and the paradox gives itself"[131] Faith is thus the consummation of the paradox. Climacus sets up an antithetical relation between the *offense* and the rise of *faith*. In the former, the understanding prevails whereas in the latter it is the paradox that thrives. Besides, faith demands that the learner steps beyond the historical dimension. According to Climacus, the historical—the Hellenic tradition—has to be suspended in order for the learner to develop faith and for the moment to become essential.

> It is at once apparent here that the historical in the more concrete sense is inconsequential; we can let ignorance step in here, let ignorance, so to speak, destroy

one fact after the other, let it historically demolish the historical—if only the moment still remains as the point of departure for the eternal, the paradox is still present.[132]

Faith overcomes the separation of the historical and the achievement of eternal happiness because it is the highest passion of subjectivity. The historical is assimilated in the experience of eternal happiness which becomes achievable through the power of faith. "in that happy passion which we call faith, the object of which is the paradox—but the paradox specifically unites the contradictories, is the eternalizing of the historical and the historicizing of the eternal."[133] Climacus does not eradicate the historical—the Hellenic perspective—after the rise of faith; rather it is suspended and repressed in order for the learner to embrace the Christian experience.[134] The learner has to be willing to accept the god under the form of a human being. This seeming absurdity constitutes the paradox. "Faith, then, must constantly cling firmly to the teacher. But in order for the teacher to be able to give the condition, he must be the god, and in order to put the learner in possession of it, he must be man. This contradiction is in turn the object of faith and is the paradox, the moment."[135] The contemporary follower ought to be consumed by faith; the rational has to be suspended in order for the follower to reach eternal happiness. By asserting these criteria, Climacus dissolves the human shape of the god as the servant. The god is essentially the synthesis of the criteria of faith. Consequently, the contemporary follower is no more privileged than the follower at second hand. For both, the human form of the god as the servant is only the historical expression of the condition for the learner to achieve eternal happiness.

Furthermore, for Climacus, faith has a distinguishing mark. Faith is essentially a direct relation between the learner and the god, as teacher. It is not accidental, that there is no mention of the Church as a mediating institution, Climacus is here assuming Protestant ethos as the basis of his discussion of faith. Climacus uses the example of Spinoza's teaching to illustrate the ideal relationship and to emphasize that the historical Spinoza is irrelevant to the learner's relation with his teaching. "If I comprehend Spinoza's teaching, then in the moment I comprehend it I am not occupied with Spinoza but with his teaching, although at some other time I am historically occupied with him."[136] Climacus does not entirely disregard the historical aspect because it provides the occasion for the relation to come about. However, the historical is sublimated in the relation because faith appropriates the historical in a non-temporal and non-historical manner. Climacus expresses that in the following definition: "The follower, however, is in faith related to that teacher in such a way that he is eternally occupied with his historical existence."[137] Hence the learner cannot forsake the historical aspect of the teacher, because the historical manifestation of the god is indeed the teaching itself. Faith consists in appropriating the historical embodiment of the god in an eternal fashion.

Faith and Kantian Idealism

In fact, the previous discussion of the relation of the understanding and the paradox, which is propaedeutic to Climacus's introduction of faith, bears an Idealist reverberation. The dichotomy that Climacus is drawing is a prevalent theme of German Idealism, which pertains to the limits of the theoretical faculties of the transcendental subject in relation to matters of faith. By so doing, Climacus is thus taking up an issue that was pervasive in German Idealism. This Idealist theme is present in Kant's Critical Idealism. The above discussion regarding understanding and faith suggests Climacus's Kantian heritage and demands further investigation. Furthermore, the account of a contemporary of Kierkegaard offers sufficient evidence to assert Kantian influence on his view of faith: "In addition to Hegel, he was influenced by Lessing, Hamman, Jacobi, and Kant, and later by the study of the Greeks, including Socrates, whom he understood in a brilliant and unique fashion and who always represented the *human* ideal for him."[138] The elaboration of the relation of the faculty of the understanding and faith is available in the *Critique of Pure Reason*. The theme of Climacus's discussion is traceable in Kant's *Preface* of the second edition of the *Critique of Pure Reason* in which he introduces the controversial position that knowledge has to be suspended to allow the emergence of faith.

Kant's second *Preface* to the *Critique of Pure Reason* starts with an assessment of the revolutionary thinking that established the apodictic basis of the natural sciences. Kant's account is intended to show the necessity to use the model of the natural sciences to bring Metaphysics to their level of certainty. For Kant, the modification in the approach to metaphysical investigation is viable because it will support and account for the rules that constitute epistemic experiences. "For this alteration in our way of thinking we can very well explain the possibility of a cognition *a priori*, and what is still more, we can provide satisfactory proofs of the laws that are the *a priori* ground of nature, as the sum total of objects of experience—which were both, impossible according to the earlier way of proceeding."[139] The Copernican revolution that Kant sets out to undertake with Metaphysics calls for a revision of the epistemological means through which knowledge and experience usually occur.

The outcome of Kant's undertaking is twofold. The first consequence is that the understanding is limited to the domain of the representations. In his words:

"But herein lies just the experiment providing a check up on the truth of the result of that first assessment of our rational cognition *a priori*, namely that such cognition reaches appearances only, leaving the thing in itself as something actual for itself but unrecognized by us."[140] This limitation is mandatory since the errors that have misled Metaphysics hitherto derive from the understanding's ventures beyond the limits of the domain of the representations. The positive outcome consists in the abolition of this source of error that constituted a hindrance to the growth of the theoretical aspect of Reason. "Hence a critique that limits the speculative use of reason is, to be sure, to that extent **negative**, but because it simultaneously removes an obstacle that limits or even threatens to wipe out the practical use of reason, this critique is also in fact **positive** and very important utility,"[141] It is through the delineation of the proper domain of epistemic experience that Kant draws the distinction between the epistemic and non-epistemic experiences.

According to Kant, the validity of epistemic experiences derives from the fact that the concepts of the understanding are able to obtain the corresponding appearances for epistemic experiences to happen. Hence epistemic experience is limited to the concepts, which are substantiated by empirical representations. The non-epistemic experiences represent the other aspect of speculative Reason. It is the activity in which the intellect freely contemplates its object without seeking to conceptualize appearances, as long as there is no inner contradiction. Kant uses the example of the notion of freedom to illustrate his point: "I can **think** freedom to myself, i.e., the representation of it at least contains no contradiction in itself, so long as our critical distinction prevails between the two ways of representing (sensible and intellectual), along with the limitation of the pure concepts of the understanding arising from it,"[142] Notions, such as the soul, God, and immortality can only be thought, since the attempt on the part of Reason to find corresponding representations will only amalgamate empirical concepts to generate empty appearances. Rational cognition determines the ground of epistemic experiences that is different from the non-epistemic contemplation of speculative Reason that lacks sensible representations. This limitation of reason is expressed in Kant's famous statement that: "Thus I had to deny **knowledge** in order to make room for faith;"[143] Knowledge and faith represent the duality of the epistemic and non-epistemic experiences.

It is at this juncture that the commonality between Kant's account and Climacus's discussion of understanding and faith become evident. Their common goal is to reflect on the way that the rational faculty can relate to God and the notions that can only be intellectually contemplated without appearances. Climacus emphasizes the need for the learner to go beyond the human shape of the god, as the servant, to allow faith to relate to divinity. According to Climacus's position, the learner's faithful relation to the divine aspect of the god is feasible only by suspending knowledge and 'making room for faith'. The ideal relation that Climacus asserts between the learner and the god is achievable through the application of Kant's above dictum. The necessity for the rise of faith at the expense of the cognitive faculties is present in both, Kant and Climacus's accounts.

Moreover, further reflection on Climacus's elaboration of the interaction of the paradox and the understanding in the rise of faith shows further similarity to Kant's account of the dynamics of the sensible representations and the concepts of the understanding. For Climacus, the occurrence of faith requires the integration of the eternal and the historical. For Climacus, the historical acquires significance in occasioning the relation to eternal happiness. That the historical become significant unless it relates to the eternal is similar to the relation of the sensible representations that are valid unless they have been subsumed under the concepts of the understanding. Climacus thinks that: "As long as the eternal and the historical remain apart from each other, the historical is only an occasion."[14] The historical—like the appearance—is thus empty unless it leads to eternal happiness, as the equivalent of the concept of the understanding in Kant's account. The subsumption of the historical under the eternal is reminiscent of the structure of Kantian experience. The priority of eternal happiness over the historical is comparable to that of the concepts over the appearances of the *noumena*, which are worthy unless they have been subsumed under the appropriate concepts. For Climacus, the subsumption happens "in that happy passion which we call faith, the object of which is the paradox—but the paradox specifically unites contradictories, is the eternalizing of the historical and the historicizing of the eternal."[14] The subsumption of the understanding under the paradox is another expression of the operation of the eternal and the historical in the rise of faith.

Climacus's account of the relation of the understanding and the paradox, which is unified through the rise of faith, draws out the influence of Kant's Critical Idealism. The Kantian influence contextualizes Climacus's project within German Idealism. It is a confirmation of Kierkegaard's reception and interpretation of the prevalent philosophical problems of his period. Hence, Ricoeur observes correctly that:

> In a sense, Kierkegaard can be regarded as part of the general movement in German Philosophy after 1840 generally known as 'the return to Kant'. The phrase 'the paradox calls for faith, not understanding' is clearly an echo of Kant's celebrated adage about the necessity 'to deny *knowledge,* in order to make room for *faith*'...Thus there is something in Kierkegaard that cannot be understood ex-

cept against a Kantian background, and something in Kant that only makes sense in terms of Kierkegaardian struggle with paradox."[145]

Climacus's discussion of the relation of the understanding and the paradox is thus an undeniable proof of the presence of Kantian influence upon Climacus's *Philosophical Fragments*.

Climacus's account of faith is further elucidated in Anti-Climacus psychological-existential discussion of the same issue in the *Sickness Unto Death* (1849). In this work, Anti-Climacus provides the structure of the dynamics of faith. The sickness unto death represents the existential predicament of subjectivity's failure to live according to God's wish. Anti-Climacus defines faith in the following: "Faith is: that the self in being itself and in willing to be itself rests transparently in God."[147] During the rise of faith, the will of God is the guiding outline of the self; it is by following God's will that the self comes to dwell peacefully in the power that created it. The paradox, as the absolutely other of the understanding, is precisely the will of God, which is expressed historically. Anti-Climacus presents the lived experience of faith under psychological-existential form, whereas, Climacus is considering faith from the cognitive aspect of the philosophical-historical.

Also, Anti-Climacus's claim that the antithesis of faith is sin is linked to Climacus's characterization of the *offense,* as the consciousness of sin. Faith is the means to overcome both, despair—the consciousness of sin—and the offense, which is the understanding's resistance to the paradox. "Sin is: *before God, or with the conception of God, in despair not to will to be oneself, or in despair to will to be oneself.*"[148] Although Anti-Climacus does not refer to the understanding explicitly as that which is carrying out the act of willing,[149] despair is the result of the existential clash that occurs between the understanding and the paradox, which occasions the passive suffering of the offense.

'Coming Into Existence' and History

The *Interlude* presents Climacus's reflection upon the traditional philosophical views of change. Climacus's analysis covers various philosophical perspectives of change and proceeds to elaborate his own on the basis of their discussion. The *Interlude* elaborates Climacus's philosophical account of the notion of change and its impact upon History. The philosophical intensity of Climacus's assessment of the philosophical accounts of the dynamics of change and the necessary leads Hannay to make the following observation: "Whatever the personal motive, the interlude is still an integral part of the overall 'argument', and its few pages present the most concentrated set of philosophical thoughts to be found in all of Kierkegaard."[150] Indeed, in these few pages, Climacus considers some accounts of change and compare them in order to point out their flaws. The strategic purpose of the assessment of change is to be a propadeutic to Climacus's account of freedom.

The question that Climacus raises about 'coming into existence' is intricate in both, structure and scope. The question is about change and the process of change; it is interested in both, the process and outcome of change. The complexity of the query derives from the fact that Climacus wishes to tackle both, of its aspects simultaneously. "How is that changed which comes into existence [*blive til*], or what is the change (χίνηις) of coming into existence [*tilblivelse*]?"[151] Climacus proceeds to establish the distinctive aspect of the change, which is intrinsic to 'coming into existence'. According to the traditional view, change presupposes a basis from which it originates. The basis is both, the bearer and that which undergoes the transformation. "All other change (άλλοίωσις) presupposes the existence of that in which change is taking place, even though the change is that of ceasing to be in existence [*at voere til*]."[152] On the other hand, 'coming into existence' is a change in being. Its main difference from the usual mode of change is that the transformation does not annihilate its basis; it is a change that does not imply the transformation of its basis. According to Climacus, 'coming into existence' implies an ontological transformation.

> If, in coming into existence, a plan is intrinsically changed, then it is not this plan that comes into existence; but if it comes into existence unchanged, what, then, is the change of coming into existence? This change, then, is not in essence [*Voesen*] but in being [*Voeren*] and is from non-existing to existing.[153]

Hence, in order to avoid running into contradiction, 'coming into existence' must have a starting point, as well. Climacus acknowledges that it is unfounded to posit change independently from an origin, he claims that: "the change of coming into existence would be absolutely different from any other change, because it would be no change at all, for every change has always presupposed a something."[154] It is in this claim that Climacus differentiates 'coming into existence' from being an *emanation* by asserting an origin. 'Coming into existence' is not an emanation because it is not a sudden generation. Thus, the source of 'coming into existence' has a unique existence: it *is* non-being. Climacus qualifies the existence of non-being as possibility, whose nature is distinct from the actual and the virtual. "But such a being that nevertheless is a non-being is possibility, and a being that is being is indeed actual being or actuality, and the change of coming into existence is the transition from possibility to actuality."[155] Then, Climacus introduces the intermediary aspect of possibility, which distinguishes 'coming into existence' from the traditional mode of change in essence.

Climacus contrasts the dynamic of 'coming into existence' with the static and immutable nature of the 'necessary'. He begins by raising the question whether the necessary undergoes the process of coming into existence? In addressing this question, Climacus aims at assessing the relation of the necessary to the possible. "Can the necessary come into existence? Coming into existence is a change, but since the necessary is always related to itself and is related to itself in the same way, it cannot be changed at all."[156] The gist of this claim is that the necessary bears its origin, as point of reference, within itself and does not involve a second party in its structure. Whereas,

> All coming into existence is a *suffering* [*Liden*], and the necessary cannot suffer, cannot suffer the suffering of actuality—namely, that the possible (not merely the possible that is excluded but even the possibility that is accepted) turns out to be nothing the moment it becomes actual, for possibility is *annihilated* by actuality. Precisely by coming into existence, everything that comes into existence demonstrates that it is not necessary, for the only thing that cannot come into existence is the necessary, because the necessary *is*.[157]

From the above claim, one may observe that Climacus means *suffering* to express the transient nature of existence. Existence is a process of undergoing. His view of existence explains actuality, which constitutes the course of action of the possible. It is noteworthy that Climacus establishes a very specific relation between possibility, as non-existence, and actuality as its concretion. The possible is thus realized as it undergoes the annihilating process of the actual.

Climacus then engages into a critique of the traditional Aristotelian notion of change. The previous differentiation between change in essence and being were meant to anticipate this analysis. Climacus's main goal is to argue that 'coming into existence', as a change in being, occurs in freedom whereas change in essence is rooted in necessity. He raises the following question: "Is not necessity, then, a unity of possibility and actuality? –what would this mean? Possibility and actuality are not different in essence but in being."[158] This question sets the ground for Climacus to delve into the implications of the answer. It leads mainly to the question regarding the rise of unity from heterogeneity. "How could there be formed from this heterogeneity a unity that would be necessity, which is not a qualification of being but of essence since the essence of the necessary is to be."[159] Climacus follows the implication of the combination of the actual and the possible to constitute the necessary.

> In such a case, possibility and actuality, in becoming necessity, would become an absolutely different essence, which is no change, and, in becoming necessity or the necessary, would become the one and only thing that precludes coming into existence, which is just as impossible as it is self-contradictory. (The Aristotelian proposition: 'it is possible [to be],' 'it is possible not [to be],' 'it is not possible [to be].'—The doctrine of true and false propositions [Epicurus] confuses the issue here, since it reflects on essence, not on being, with the result that nothing is achieved along that path with regard to defining the future.)[160]

For Climacus, the main problem with the Aristotelian view of the fusion of the possible and the actual in the constitution of the necessary is that it prevents authentic change; it does not freely yield existence, but only brings about a different configuration of the essence. For Climacus, Aristotle confines the necessary to stasis. Its stagnant nature opposes any sort of transformation. "Necessity stands all by itself. Nothing whatever comes into existence by way of necessity, no more than necessity comes into existence or anything in coming into existence becomes the necessary."[161]

Climacus is here proceeding very strategically to delineate the flaws of the Aristotelian view of change. His definition of actuality, as the course of action of possibility, becomes relevant at this stage of the assessment. Climacus believes that the actual is not superior to the possible. For Climacus, the actual and the possible are equal because the former lies in the fleeting process of that which is annihilated and the latter is ascribed to the virtual. They are similar in virtue of their lack of permanence.

> The actual is no more necessary than the possible, for the necessary is absolutely different from both. (Aristotle's theory of two kinds of the possible in relation to the necessary. His mistake is to begin with the thesis that everything necessary is possible. To avoid contradictory—indeed, self-contradictory—statements about the necessary, he makes shift by formulating two kinds of the possible instead of discovering that his first thesis is incorrect, since the possible cannot be predicated of the necessary.)[162]

The possible cannot derive from the necessary because the latter is stagnant by nature. Consequently, the transition of the possible through the actual, as *suffering*, can only happen in freedom, which is the natural antithesis of necessity. "The change of coming into existence is actuality; the transition takes place in freedom...All coming into existence occurs in freedom, not by way of necessity. Nothing comes into existence by way of a ground, but everything by way of a cause."[163] It is at this juncture that Climacus lets it slip that his critique is aimed at Hegel's account of the relation between existence, ground, and necessity in the *Logic*. Climacus has been developing his criticism of Hegel through Aristotle's account, which he assumes to underlie the Hegelian view. Stack comments on the underlying intention of Climacus's discussion in the following statement: "What he sought in the writings of Trendelenburg and Aristotle was a theoretical means of avoiding the Hegelian assumption of *necessary* dialectical developments while, at the same time, retaining a dialectical interpretation of the various existential dimensions of human life."[164]

The accuracy of this claim is verifiable through Climacus's discussion of the manifestation of freedom. Climacus refutes the determinism that is inherent to causality. Causes seem to be necessary, for Climacus, because reflection fails to acknowledge the free path from which they emerge. "The intervening causes are misleading in that the coming into existence appears to be necessary; the truth about them is that they, as having themselves come into existence, *definitively* point back to a freely acting cause. As soon as coming into existence is definitively reflected upon, even an inference from natural law is not evidence of the necessity of any coming into existence."[165] Hence, it is retrospective considerations that mistakenly associate the free act with necessity; the error consists in failing to contemplate the various alternatives and their outcomes. For Climacus, freedom is absolute because each free act derives from a pure freedom and leads to a series of subsequent free acts as well. There is no determined effect since the outcome of a free event is the occasion for another free event to come about. "So also with manifestations of freedom, as soon as one refused to be deceived by its manifestations but reflects on its coming into existence."[166] Climacus thinks that it is a mirage of reflection to posit necessity as the basis of natural occurrences.

Climacus turns his focus toward the historical, which he categorizes under what has 'come into existence' to demonstrate that the historical is situated within a broader frame, which itself comes from an absolutely free act. The previous discussion of the difference between the change of 'coming into existence' and the 'necessary' was intended to set up the basis for Climacus's account of History. For Climacus, History differs from the necessary in virtue of its mutable nature. "Everything that has come into existence is *eo ipso* historical, for even if no further historical predicate can be applied to it, the crucial predicate of the historical can still be predicated—namely, that it has come into existence."[167] The distinctive feature of History is that it is *simultaneous*. "Something whose coming into existence is a simultaneous coming into existence (*Nebeneinander* [side-by-side], space) has no other History than this, but nature, even when perceived in this manner (*en masse*), apart from what a more ingenious view calls the History of nature in a special sense, does have a History."[168] Climacus's cryptic statement expresses the inseparable relation between nature and History, which can become manifest through each other. Climacus is suggesting that on the one hand, nature acquires its autonomy as the *natural* via History. On the other hand, History is able to unfold, as the historical, through nature as its basis. Climacus pushes his position further by establishing nature as the concrete setting of the historical. Nature represents the spatial bearer of historical events. For Climacus, nature itself did not come about in a consecutive order since that would subjugate it to a necessary process. The fact that nature is a simultaneous 'coming into existence' exhibits its freedom and its transition from non-being into being. However, for Climacus, the contradiction that arises from asserting that nature has a history is that: "the historical is the past (for the present on the border with the future has not as yet become historical); how, then, can nature, although immediately present, be said to be historical—unless one is thinking of that ingenious view?"[169] Nature is the sole phenomenon that is both, past and present. It is past in virtue of its historical role and present through its availability to sensory perceptions. The paradoxical relation of nature with time shows that its involvement with the temporal is accidental and not necessary. For Climacus, nature is essentially *atemporal*.

> The difficulty arises because nature is too abstract to be dialectical, in the stricter sense of the word, with respect to time. Nature's imperfection is that it does not have a History in another sense, and its perfection is that it nevertheless has an intimation of it (namely, that it has come into existence, which is the past; that it exists, which is the present).[170]

Climacus's attempt to secure the non-historical origin of nature has an ulterior aim, mainly to establish it as the manifestation of the eternal. Nature assures the freedom of History because it stands as the absolutely free point of reference. The freedom of nature denies all necessity within the structure of History. Moreover, the eternal is, for Climacus, the absolutely free; the eternal is pure freedom. Climacus states that: "It is, however, the perfection of the eternal to have no History, and of all that is, only the eternal has absolutely no History."[171] Consequently, nature is the proper manifestation of the eternal since it does not have a History. At this juncture, Climacus establishes the priority of the eternal over the historical through nature's non-historical origin. The historical is thus reconciled with the broader framework of the eternal.

> The coming into existence that here is shared with the coming into existence of nature is a possibility, a possibility that for nature is its whole actuality. But this distinctively historical coming into existence is nevertheless within a coming into existence—this must be grasped securely at all times. The more special historical coming into existence comes into existence by way of a freely acting cause, which in turn definitively points to an absolutely freely acting cause.[172]

The historical is distinct from nature, its absolute basis, because it is mediated through time. According to Climacus's standpoint, the seeming intimacy between nature and time happens through the mediation of History by time. Reflection incorrectly ascribes to nature what really belongs to History.

Climacus shifts his attention to the role of immutability in the structure of the past. He begins by questioning the immutability of the past, which is compared to necessity. Climacus's investigation of the nature of unchangeableness is carried out from the perspective of the past and necessity. Unchangeableness turns out to be twofold. The unchangeableness of the past is different from that of necessity, because it falls within the temporal segment, which belongs to the historical. "The unchangeableness of the past has been brought about by a change, by the change of coming into existence, but an unchangeableness such as that does not exclude all change, since it has not excluded this one"[173] The unchangeableness of the past is the outcome of the transition of non-being into being, which for Climacus occurs in freedom. For Climacus, the main basis of the unchangeable nature of the past is that past events cannot be undone. "What has happened has happened the way it happened; thus it is unchangeable...The unchangeableness of the past is that its actual 'thus and so' cannot become different, but from this does it follow that its possible 'how' could not have been different?"[174]

On the other hand, the immutability of necessity consists in the fact that it is independent of all changes. The necessary is essentially immutable. Necessity relates to itself absolutely and does not have any external determinant. "But the unchangeableness of the necessary—that is constantly related to itself and is related to itself in the same way and excludes all change—is not satisfied with the unchangeableness of the past,"[175] Necessity differs from the past not merely because the former relates to itself absolutely, but also because its 'how' or structure could not have been otherwise. However, Climacus anticipates the difficulty that arises by positing the unchangeableness of the past within the domain of freedom. The difficulty is mainly to account for the transition of freedom into the past, the way in which past events become unchangeable. For Climacus, the passage of the possible into the unchangeableness of the past happens through the motion of the future toward the past. Climacus makes the following claim to emphasize this fact: "To want to predict the future (prophesy) and to want to understand the necessity of the past are altogether identical, and only the prevailing fashion makes the one seem more plausible than the other to a particular generation."[176] Climacus is here attempting to establish a direct relation between the future and the past. The former represents the bearer of possibility, which passes into the unchangeableness of the past. The real incentive of Climacus's analysis is to demarcate the role of freedom in the structure of the historical. This fact becomes evident in the claim below:

> If the past had become necessary, then it would not belong to freedom anymore that is, belong to that in which it came into existence. Freedom would be in dire straits, something to laugh about and to weep over, since it would bear responsibility for what did not belong to it,[177]

Climacus returns to the relation between nature and History to suggest that History is the inherent extension of the former. Nature, as the eternal and absolutely free has two facades; it is manifestly present to the sensory perceptions and also represents the past under its *historical costume*. "Nature as spatial determination exists only immediately. Something that is dialectical with respect to time has an intrinsic duplexity [*Dobbelthed*], so that after having been present it can endure as a past."[178] The issue that arises is that the eternal, under its historical costume, requires a different means of apprehension than the sensory perceptions. The historical manifestation of the eternal has to be grasped through a different organon that is able to grapple with the resulting uncertainty of past events. Climacus regards the uncertain characteristic of the historical as definitive. "Only in this contradiction between certainty and uncertainty, the *discrimen* [distinctive mark] of something that has come into existence and thus also of the past, is the past understood."[179] History is so elusive to immediate grasp that Climacus boldly asserts that the attempt to appropriate the past complies with the structure of prophesying. Both, the past and the future are equally elusive to direct grasp. "One who apprehends the past, a *historico-philosophus*, is therefore a prophet in reverse. That he is a prophet simply indicates that the basis of the certainty of the past is the uncertainty regarding it in the same sense as there is uncertainty regarding the future,"[180] Climacus's view suggests that to historicize is to strive to overcome uncertainty; the same way predicting the future wishes to defeat the uncertain. Both, History and prophesying the future represent anxiety over uncertainty and despair before the unknown.

Climacus takes up the means through which the past can be appropriated. History, unlike an object of perception, cannot be pointed out; History is not tangible. The way to relate to the historical is to posit that it has 'come into existence'; it is 'present' only as having 'come into existence'. Climacus explains: "Immediate sensation and immediate cognition cannot deceive. This alone indicates that the historical cannot become the object of sense perception or of immediate cognition, because the historical has in itself that very illusiveness that is the illusiveness of coming into existence."[181] The conviction that the historical has come into existence is precisely what removes it from the domain of immediacy. Consequently, the medium to grasp the historical must be intrinsically able to prevail over the uncertain aspect. Climacus elaborates:

> It is clear, then, that the organ for the historical must be formed in likeness to this, must have within itself the corresponding something by which in its certitude it continually annuls the incertitude that corresponds to the uncertainty of coming into existence—a double uncertainty: the nothingness of non-being and the annihilated possibility, which is also the annihilation of every other possibility. This is precisely the nature of belief [*tro*], for continually present as the nullified in the certitude of belief is the incertitude that in every way corresponds to the uncertainty of coming into existence. Thus, belief believes what it does not see; it does not believe that the star exists, for that it sees, but it believes that the star has come into existence.[182]

One of the privileges of belief is that it accepts the 'coming into existence' as absolute and by the same token does not rule out the possibility that it could have been otherwise. Thus, belief adheres to what is elusive to sensory perceptions and is simultaneously aware that its object is the expression of freedom, which occasions other free acts.

> In contrast, it is now readily apparent that belief is not a knowledge but an act of freedom, an expression of will it believes the coming into existence and has annulled in itself the incertitude that corresponds to the nothingness of that which is not. It believes the 'thus and so' of that which has come into existence and has annulled in itself the possible 'how' of that which has come into existence, and without denying the possibility of another 'thus and so,' the 'thus and so' of that which has come into existence is nevertheless most certain for belief.[183]

Climacus's strategy posits belief outside of the domain of the cognitive faculties. The attitude of belief does not depend on the object of sensory perception, but *wills* the certainty of the object's having 'come into existence'. It is on this basis that Climacus declares that belief eradicates doubt and does not guarantee knowledge. Unlike knowledge, belief does not reach conclusions but is resolute in the face of its object. "The conclusion of belief is no conclusion [*Slutning*] but a resolution [*Beslutning*], and thus doubt is excluded...Belief is the opposite of doubt...belief is a sense for coming into existence, and doubt is a protest against any conclusion that wants to go beyond immediate sensation and immediate knowledge."[184] Hence, given that belief does not conclude, then one cannot err by believing. Climacus excludes the possibility of deception from belief by arguing that it is merely resolute. Belief has a creative and generative power that is foreign to cognitive knowledge.

Climacus's in-depth analysis is meant to establish that belief is the proper organon for both, the contemporary and follower at second hand to relate to the god. Climacus aims at showing that belief, by being able to accept the 'coming into existence', is capable of transcending temporal distance. By the means of belief, the follower at second hand and the contemporary follower become equally close to the god. "Belief and coming into existence correspond to each other and involve the annulled qualifications of being, the past and the future, and the present only insofar as it is regarded under annulled qualification of being as that which has come into existence."[185] The fact that belief does not operate on the basis of sensory data nullifies the phenomenal aspect of the god for the contemporary follower and follower at second hand. Moreover, the phenomenal aspect of the god can only mislead the contemporary follower because the god is to be grasped through a different medium than the cognitive, mainly faith. The god is a possibility that faith has to renew through each generation in willing it into existence by the means of belief. Climacus summarizes the paradoxical aspect of the god as a historical fact and how it relates to the contemporary and follower at second hand:

> So, then, that historical fact remains. It has no immediate contemporary, because it is historical to the first power (faith in the ordinary sense [belief]); it has no immediate contemporary to the second power, since it is based on a contradiction (faith in the eminent sense). But for those who are very different with respect to time, this latter equality absorbs the differences among those who are temporally different in the first sense.[186]

Critique of Hegelian Possibility

The polemic tone of the *Interlude* calls for further consideration. Climacus's development of the dynamics of possibility, actuality, and the necessary has a polemical purpose. The above exposition aims simultaneously at critiquing the Hegelian account of possibility, actuality, and necessity in the *Logic*. In order to further understand the incentive of Climacus's standpoint, the Hegelian position on these notions needs to be developed. In Hegel's *Logic*, the section on *Actuality* provides an account of possibility that characterizes it as thorough indeterminacy. Hegel argues that the possible is the bearer of all that could pass into existence; pure possibility is unbound because what it bears has not yet related to anything other than itself. For Hegel, the only inherent limit of the realm of possibility is that it does not contain any self-contradiction. "According to the first, the merely positive side, therefore, possibility is the mere form determination of *identity-with-self* or the form of essentiality. As such it is the relationless, indeterminate receptacle for everything whatever. In the sense of this formal possibility *everything is possible that is not self-contradictory*; hence the realm of possibility is a boundless multiplicity."[187] The possible is that which is awaiting concrete expression. It requires the external circumstances in order to become manifest; otherwise it merely remains in its simplicity and free of all distinctions. Each possibility is entitled to a corresponding form of being as long as it is not prevented by self-contradiction. The possible is a potential; it represents a form that has not yet been hypostatized. In its potential state the possible has formal actuality; the formal actuality of the possible constitutes its embryonic stage.

> Here at the same time is more precisely expressed, how far possibility is actuality. For possibility is not yet *all* actuality; no question has yet arisen of real and absolute actuality; it is at first only that possibility which first presented itself, namely, formal possibility which has determined itself as being *only* possibility, and is thus formal actuality which is only *being* or *Existence* in general. Everything possible has therefore in general a *being* or an *Existence*.[188]

Given that it is still hollow, the formal actuality of the possible has not yet achieved concretion and is thus unable to eradicate the possibility of its antithesis. The antithesis of the formal actual enjoys the same level of possibility. Hegel qualifies the first stage of the actual and possible as being contingent. "This unity of possibility and actuality is contingency. The contingent is an actual that at the same time is determined as merely possible, whose other or opposite equally is. This actuality is having the value of a positedness or of possibility."[189] The contingent stands as a mere projection of the possible. In its formality, the contingent is paradoxical, for Hegel, since it is both, groundless and grounded. It is groundless because it has not yet been mediated and belongs to mere potentiality. On the other hand, it has a ground since it stands as a projection of the possible; it is grounded within the possible that it posits.

> The contingent therefore presents two sides. First, in so far as it has possibility *immediately* in it—or what is the same thing, in so far as possibility is sublated in it—it is neither *positedness* nor is it mediated, but is *immediate* actuality; it has no ground...But secondly, the contingent is the actual as a merely possible or as a *positedness;* thus the possible, too, as the formal in-itself is only a positedness. Hence neither is in and for itself but has its true reflection-into-self in another, *or it has a ground.*[190]

The transition of the possible into its formal actuality gives rise to the necessary. Necessity, according to Hegel, derives from the outcome of the dialectic of the possible and formal actuality. The necessary is the juncture at which the possible passes into being. The formal actual is still latent into the necessary, except that it is different from its concretion in being. "The contingent, therefore, is necessary because the actual is determined as a possible, hence its immediacy is sublated and repelled into the *ground* or the *in-itself,* and the *grounded,* and also because this its *possibility,* the *ground-relation* is simply sublated and posited as being...Thus actuality in that which is distinguished from it, namely possibility, is identical with itself. As this identity it is necessity."[191] The necessary is higher than formal actuality because by achieving expression in being, it eliminates the possibility of its antithesis. The necessary is not the contingent because its *being* vanquishes the being of its other. Hegel accentuates the fixed characteristic of the necessary in the following claim: "What is necessary *cannot be otherwise;* but what is simply *possible* can...Therefore what is really possible can no longer be otherwise; under the particular conditions and circumstances something else cannot follow."[192] The constellation of the external conditions assures the immutability of the necessary, which has succeeded over other possibilities and asserted its differences from other determinations.

Climacus's contention is aimed at Hegel's characterization of the necessary as coming to be via the activities of the possible and the formal actual. Climacus resists the Hegelian position because he holds that the necessary is essentially unchangeable and independent from all mutability; for Climacus, the necessary *is.* Climacus thinks that, unlike Hegel, the possible and the formal actual are indeed different in being. For Climacus, being belongs essentially to the necessary, the difference between the possible and formal actual cannot yield a new unity, which Hegel posits as the necessary. Climacus's standpoint is that in allowing the possible and formal actual to yield the necessary, Hegel transforms their essence, which is no longer able to occasion change, given that the necessary prohibits all changes. Climacus summarizes his criticism of the Hegelian position in the following:

> Is not necessity, then, a unity of possibility and actuality?—What would this mean? Possibility and actuality are not different in essence but in being. How could there be formed from this heterogeneity a unity that would be necessity, which is not a qualification of being but of essence, since the essence of the necessary is to be. In such a case, possibility and actuality, in becoming necessity, would become an absolutely different essence, which is no change, and, in becoming necessity, would become the one and only thing that precludes coming into existence, which is just as impossible as it is self-contradictory.[193]

Climacus believes that Hegel erroneously posits necessity within the domain of mutable being, by positing it in the relation of the possible and formal actual. The necessary is indifferent toward the being that results from changes because it is essentially immutable being.

Faith and the Occasion

The structure of chapter five is remarkable because Climacus wishes to provide an account of the difference between the contemporary follower and the follower at second hand upon the basis of their similarity. The chapter unfolds on the common basis of the follower at second hand and the contemporary follower to elicit their dissimilarity. The common starting point is the manifestation of the eternal in the historical through the god. Besides, it is in relation to the god that the category of follower derives its relevance. The leading question of the chapter is: How does the follower at second hand appropriate the historical expression of the eternal? Climacus is setting out to ponder the apparent disadvantage of the follower at second hand in relation to the seeming insoluble historical distance between the coming of the god and the nineteenth century. For Climacus: "The question seems imperative, likewise the question's claim on an explanation of the potential difficulties involved in defining the similarity and difference between a *follower* at second hand and a contemporary follower."[194] Thus, the contemporary follower enjoys the privilege of having physical evidence that can corroborate the attempt to appropriate the god. It is precisely with the intention to show the insignificance of the physico-historical appearance for the appropriation of the god that Climacus will do away with the difference between secondary and contemporary followers by stressing the necessity of each generation of followers to resurrect the god through faith and belief.

Hence Climacus starts his reflections on the followers at second hand by asserting his intention to focus upon them independently of the contemporary followers. The followers at second hand stand as an independent category which in relating to itself is both, similar to and distinct from itself. Thus, Climacus's investigation of the followers at second hand does not have to comply with systematic continuity because it does not relate to any antithetical factor. Climacus summarizes this fact in the following claims:

> Here, then, we shall not reflect on the relation of the secondary follower to the contemporary follower, but the difference to be reflected upon is of such a kind that the similarity (in contrast to another group) of those differing among themselves remains, for the difference that is different only within itself remains within the similarity to itself. Therefore, it is not arbitrary to break off wherever one so desires, for the relative difference here is no sorites from which the quality is supposed to appear by a *coup des mains* [sudden stroke], since it is within the specific quality.[195]

The non-syllogistic nature of Climacus's endeavor allows for arbitrary division in dealing with the issue, since it does not have to be determined in relation to any opposite. The fact that Climacus is focusing upon the followers at second hand alone allows that he may begin the investigation of the issue at any juncture that he deems suitable. Climacus states that: "Opposites show up most strongly when placed together, and therefore we choose here the first generation of secondary followers and the latest (the boundary of the given *spatium* [period], the eighteen hundred and forty-three years), and we shall be as brief as possible, for we are speaking not historically but algebraically, and we have no desire to divert or fascinate anyone with the enchantments of multiplicity."[196] Climacus's main concern is to emphasize the unifying similarity upon which the differentiating process is feasible. Climacus introduces a duality within the category of the followers at second hand; the first and latest generations are the two constituents that result from it.

The privileged position of the first generation of followers at second hand is threatened by the possibility of misusing faith to appropriate the god historically. Such misuse is plausible, according to Climacus, because of the historical proximity of the members of this generation to previous sources that have had trustworthy information about the life of the god. "This generation has (relatively) the advantage of being closer to the immediate certainty, of being closer to acquiring exact and reliable information about what happened from men whose reliability can be verified in other ways."[197] However, one question arises because the first generation's relation to these sources contradicts Climacus's previous declaration to consider the followers at second hand independently of any other category. Climacus seems to have anticipated this objection because he gives the example of a member of the first generation who strives to appropriate the god via the means of judicious historical testimonies. But, this approach errs, for Climacus, because the historical accounts merely provide an approximation to the god. Climacus describes the reaction of the god toward this fact:

> Would not the god rather smile at him for wanting to obtain under duress in this manner what cannot be purchased for money but also cannot be taken by force? Even if that fact which we are discussing were a simple historical fact, difficulties would not fail to arise if he tried to reach absolute agreement on every small detail—a matter of enormous importance to him because the passion of faith, that is, the passion that is just as intense as faith, had taken a wrong turn toward the purely historical.[198]

Despite the rigor of such undertaking the god remains elusive to it. Besides, the painstaking and obsessive nature of the misappropriation already hints at the fact that it is a desperate attempt to appropriate the god. The uncompromising pursuit of facts is already an indication of the foreboding that the god's existence has an excess over the historical.

Climacus thinks that the meticulous gathering of historical information may even cancel the privilege that the contemporary followers had in virtue of their physico-historical co-existence with the god. "He [member of the first generation] would have attained a certainty even greater than that of the contemporary who saw and heard, for the latter would readily discover that he sometimes did not see and sometimes saw wrongly,"[199] Climacus undermines the historical role of the contemporary follower by pointing out the possibility that a later generation may have a more thorough account of the god. The certainty that the historical makes available to the contemporary follower may equally be misleading. For Climacus, the coming of the god is a wonder which is obvious only to faith and belief. The role of the historical is to occasion the need to embrace the god through the means of belief. "In other words, awareness is by no means partial to faith, as if faith proceeded as a simple consequence of awareness. The advantage is that one enters into a state in which the decision manifests itself ever more clearly. This is an advantage, and this is the only advantage that means anything—indeed, it means so much that it is terrifying and is in no way an easy comfort."[200] The discomforting aspect of historical awareness consists in its call to the follower to go beyond the historical by *believing* in the existence of the god. Consequently, the importance of the historical consists in the fact that it creates the need for the follower to overcome it.

On the other hand, Climacus thinks that the latest generation of followers, unlike the first generation, does not have the opportunity to collect historical data from trustworthy sources. The latest generation encounters the historical impact of the coming of the god; they meet the historical traces of the god; the latest generation does not rely upon the direct verbal accounts of the god. They belong to the age that has come about as the result of the historical expression of the eternal.

> This generation is a long way from the jolt, but, on the other hand, it does have the consequences to hold on to, has the probability proof of the outcome, has directly before it the consequences with which that fact presumably must have embraced everything, has close at hand the probability proof from which there nevertheless is no direct transition to faith, since, as has been shown, faith is by no means partial to
> probability—to say that about faith would be slander.[201]

The logical assurance that the latest generation derives from the consequences of the existence of the god is merely cognitive. Climacus thinks that such logical certainty does not provide the latest generation the transforming condition; it is impotent for the appropriation of the god, which can only occur through faith.

> Even if one considers the consequences purely logically—that is, in the form of immanence—it still remains true that a consequence can be defined only as identical and homogeneous with its cause, but least of all as having a transforming power. To have the consequences in front of one's nose, then, is just as dubious an advantage as to have immediate certainty, and someone who takes the consequences immediately and directly is just as deceived as someone who takes immediate certainty for faith.[202]

Thus, the latest generation is equally likely to misuse the passion of faith. The main difference is that the contemporary follower may misuse faith by appropriating historical data of the existence of the god whereas the follower at second hand's misuse occurs in deriving logical consequences from the historical accounts. Climacus emphasizes that the god resists both, historical and logical grasp.

Another reason that Climacus gives for the unsuitability of logical certainty is that the starting point is different from the nature of the usual first premise of syllogisms. Whereas, the first premise of syllogisms is usually in agreement with the cognitive faculties of the logician, the premise of the consequences that the latest generation experiences is the paradox and eludes cognitive grasp. "But, humanly speaking, consequences built upon a paradox are built upon the abyss, and the total content of the consequences, which is handed down to the single individual only under the agreement that it is by virtue of a paradox, is not to be passed on like real estate, since the whole thing is in suspense."[203] Climacus reinforces the algebraic nature of the relation, which opposes syllogistic continuity. Moreover, the paradoxical premise alters the consequences for each generation, since the paradox cannot be passed down in a universal fashion. The fundamental limitation of the logical process is that it belongs to the quantitative and historical and can never result in the qualitative aspect of the leap of faith. Climacus grants imagination the ability to freelance upon the historical basis of the consequences, but also asserts its inability to arrive at the qualitative in the following mythological metaphor: "The quantitative makes for the manifoldness of life and is continually weaving its multicolored tapestry. It is like that one goddess of fate who sat spinning, but then it holds true that thought, like the other goddess of fate, sees to clipping the thread—something (apart from the metaphor) that ought to take place every time the quantitative wants to constitute quality."[204]

Then, Climacus proceeds to elaborate the various alternatives of the followers at second hand to relate to the god, and elaborates their shortcomings. The first one is to regard the coming of the god as a mere historical event. Accordingly, this position privileges the historical situation of the contemporary followers for their historical co-existence with the god. For Climacus, time is the decisive factor in this context since it determines the closeness of each to the god. "(a) If that fact is regarded as a simple historical fact, then being contemporary counts for something, and it is an advantage to be contemporary (understood more explicitly as stated in Chapter 4), or to be as close as possible, or to able to assure oneself of the reliability of the contemporaries, etc. Every historical fact is only a relative fact, and therefore it is entirely appropriate for the relative power, time, to decide the relative fates of people with respect to contemporaneity."[205] The second option is to consider the manifestation of the god as an eternal fact. Under this option historical certainty is irrelevant, and every generation enjoys equal closeness to the god. However, this characterization is not from the standpoint of faith because the historical and faith share a proportionate relation. Hence, it is really the cognitive awareness of the eternal nature of the god. "(b) If that fact is an eternal fact, then every age is equally close to it—but, please note, not in faith, for faith and the historical are entirely commensurate, and thus it is only an accommodation to a less correct use of language for me to use the word 'fact,' which is taken from the historical."[206] The third possibility is to accept the god as absolute. To posit the god as absolute automatically rules out the role of time in assessing each generation's closeness to him. For Climacus, the inadequacy of the third possibility is that it completely jettisons the historical aspect of the god. It only acknowledges the absolute aspect. Climacus explains:

> (c) If that fact is an absolute fact, or, to define it even more exactly, if that fact is what we have set forth, then it is a contradiction for time to be able to apportion the relations of people to it—that is, apportion them in a crucial sense, for whatever can be apportioned essentially by time is *eo ipso* not the absolute because that would imply that the absolute itself is a *casus* in life, a status in relation to something else, whereas the absolute, although declinable in all the *casibus* of life, is continually the same and in its continual relation to something else is continually *status absolutus*. But the absolute fact is indeed also historical. If we pay no attention to that, then all out hypothetical discussion is demolished to that, then we are speaking only of an eternal fact. The absolute fact is a historical fact and as such the object of faith. The historical aspect must indeed be accentuated.[207]

For Climacus the correct approach is to consider the god as eternal with the addendum that it is an occasion for belief to arise. Climacus associates the historical with the eternal for faith by positing the coming of the god for the contemporary followers and the accounts of later witnesses as having one common purpose—to be the occasion for being a genuine follower. "Just as the historical becomes the occasion for the contemporary to become a follower—by receiving the condition, please note, from the god himself (for otherwise we speak Socratically)—so the report of the contemporaries becomes the occasion for everyone coming later to become a follower—by receiving the condition, please note, from the god himself."[208] But, Climacus's position is not without a warning. Climacus is concerned that the process of giving the occasion for faith to the latest generation might result in mistaking the witness for the god or the object of worship. To prevent this from taking place, Climacus suggests the maieutic approach of Socratic teaching for its ability to guide the learner without edifying the teacher. "But if the one who comes later also receives the condition from the god, then the Socratic relation will return—but, please note, within the total difference consisting of that fact and the relation of the single individual (the contemporary and the one who came later) to the god."[209] Thus, the individual's relation to the god via Socratic teaching sets the basis for the god to give the condition anew each time. This method reincarnates the god for every generation. Nevertheless, Climacus is loyal to the transcendence of the Hellenic because it is essentially the god who reaches out to each individual by means of the Socratic. "Our project went beyond Socrates only in that it placed the god in relation to the single individual, but who indeed would dare come to Socrates with such nonsense—that a human being is a god in relation to another human being?"[210] Climacus seems to believe that the Christian perspective would be sheer absurdity to the Greek individual. Socratic teaching can only be conducive to the rise of the Christian experience; it reaches its apex at the juncture where Christianity starts.

At this phase of the development of the issue of the followers at second hand, that Climacus sets out to explore from the perspective of differences within the similar, the question of the followers at second hand turns out to be a pseudo-issue. The initial difference between the followers at second hand and contemporary followers is cancelled out because the god is the exemplar through which one becomes a genuine Christian independently of their historical closeness or distance. Climacus reveals the futility of the question: "But If he has understood it, he will also understand that there is not and cannot be any question of a follower at second hand, for the believer (and only he, after all, is a follower) continually has the *autopsy* of faith; he does not see with the eyes of others and sees only the same as every believer sees—with the eyes of faith."[211] The ideal way for someone from a previous generation to assist another from a later generation is to invite her to believe in the god on her own terms. Climacus states that: "He can tell someone who comes later that he himself has believed that fact; this actually is not a communication at all (that there is no immediate contemporaneity and that the fact is based upon a contradiction indicate this) but merely an occasion."[212] A few lines further Climacus boldly asserts that: "Only the person who personally receives the condition from the god (which completely corresponds to the requirement that one relinquish the understanding and on the other hand is the only authority that corresponds to faith), only that person believes."[213] Each individual is expected to relate in faith to the god alone; for Climacus, the self has to die to the cognitive faculties in order to be born again through the god. The suspension of the understanding and the uselessness of the logical relation to the god are the primary requirements of the Christian ethos that Climacus is asserting. In the conclusion, Climacus discloses his goal: "As is well known, Christianity is the only historical phenomenon that despite the historical—indeed, precisely by means of the historical—has wanted to be the single individual's point of departure for his eternal consciousness, has wanted to interest him otherwise than merely historically, has wanted to base his happiness on his relation to something historical."[214] Mulhall's comment clarifies Climacus's position further:

Since, however, it is also part of the Christian message as Climacus understands it that human beings are incapable of establishing such a relationship by means of their own efforts—since human nature is sinful, and so not so much oriented away from the truth as mired in untruth—they must rely upon Christ not only to initiate that personal relationship but also to put them in a position from which such an orientation to the truth is even possible. In short, human beings require conversion or re-birth as well as re-orientation, and both, require grace - a gratuitous, entirely undeserved and purely loving move on the part of Christ to come into contact with them.[315]

The conclusion of Chapter five is the culmination of Climacus's algebraic undertaking to answer the question: Whether the historical can be the starting point for the learner's eternal happiness. The answer to this question is the outcome of a series of notions that Climacus elaborates in each phase of the project. Moreover, the implicit demonstration, which is to transcend Socrates as a central figure of Kierkegaard's first major work, is successfully carried out. Climacus starts with the Hellenic tradition, then introduces the historical rupture, as the introduction of the eternal and ends with the assertion of the Christian experience, which represents the apex of Western consciousness. Climacus gives more details in the *Moral*:

> This project indisputably goes beyond the Socratic, as is apparent at every point. Whether it is therefore more true than the Socratic is an altogether different question, one that cannot be decided in the same breath, inasmuch as a new organ has been assumed here: faith; and a new presupposition: the consciousness of sin; an a new decision: the moment; and a new teacher: the god in time. Without these, I really would not have dared to present myself for inspection before that ironist who has been admired for millennia, whom I approach with as much ardent enthusiasm as anyone. But to go beyond Socrates when one nevertheless says essentially the same as he, only not nearly so well—that, at least, is not Socratic.[316]

Lessing's Account of Christ's Teachings

The issue of the role of History in Christianity that Climacus attempts to solve in the above exposition was a frequent theme among theologians and philosophers of the eighteenth and nineteenth century. The relation of historical certainty and faith in Christianity was the topic of several academic debates across Europe. Although Climacus does not explicitly mention any of his predecessors and contemporaries' views on the issue, the chapter is indeed a philosophical-theological conversation with one of the key figures that had previously pondered the problem of historical certainty and faith in the instructions and deeds of Christ. Throughout Chapter five, Climacus is conversing implicitly with Gotthold Lessing. Lessing addresses the same theme as Climacus's discussion and often uses similar terminologies in his essay: *On the Proof of the Spirit and of Power.*

Lessing's goal in this essay is to assess the medium through which the teachings of Christ ought to be appropriated because as historical truths they can not be proven absolutely. Lessing starts the essay by distinguishing between first hand experiences of prophecies and miracles from the reports of others regarding prophecies and miracles. For Lessing, first hand experiences of the prophecies and miracles of Jesus Christ can only compel one to devote more attention to him. In his words:

> Fulfilled prophecies, which I myself experience, are one thing; fulfilled prophecies, of which I know only from History that others say they have experienced are another...Miracles, which I see with my own eyes, and which I have the opportunity to verify for myself, are one thing; miracles, of which I know only from History that others say they have seen them and verified them, are another.[217]

Lessing thinks that being a witness of the accomplishments of Christ makes one more attentive. This fact is noteworthy because Lessing wishes to stress that one who has had first hand experiences of the deeds of Christ does not necessarily become faithful. In addition, the distinction that Lessing draws in the above claim is similar to Climacus's differentiation between the contemporary followers and the followers at second hand. In Lessing's context, those who have experienced the prophecies and miracles correspond to the contemporary followers of Climacus, as historically co-existing with the god. On the other hand, the ones that received historical reports share the same position as the first and latest generation of the followers at second hand in Climacus's discussion.

Then, Lessing raises an important question concerning what may prevent one from appropriating the prophecies and miracles of Christ: "Or: if I even now experienced that prophecies referring to Christ or the Christian religion, of whose priority in time I have long been certain, were fulfilled in a manner admitting no dispute; if even now miracles were done by believing Christians which I had to recognize as true miracles: what could prevent me from accepting this proof of the spirit and of power, as the apostle calls it?"[218] This question strengthens Lessing's position that first hand or being a contemporary witness of Christ's prophecies and accomplishments is not sufficient to appropriate them. The answer to this question sheds light on Climacus's relentless attempt to transcend the attitude of the Greeks.

In the last instance Origen was quite right in saying that in this proof of the spirit and of power the Christian religion was able to provide a proof of its own more divine than all Greek dialectic. For in his time there was still 'the power to do miraculous things which still continued' among those who lived after Christ's precept; and if he had undoubted examples of this, then if he was not to deny his own senses he had of necessity to recognize that proof of the spirit and of power.[119]

By referring to 'Greek dialectic', Lessing means the cognitive faculties. It is important to note that a similar view of 'Greek dialectic' is present in Climacus's account of the understanding that he posits as the dominant organon of the Hellenic tradition. It is by transcending the understanding—the epitome of Greek's intellectual life—that one can embrace Christianity and become faithful. For Lessing, the historical data of the prophecies and miracles have been purged of their persuasive force by a medium that is made explicit in Climacus's project. "These, the prophecies fulfilled before my eyes, the miracles that occur before my eyes are immediate in their effect. But those—the reports of fulfilled prophecies and miracles, have to work through a medium which takes away all their force."[220] The medium that Lessing has in mind is time which Climacus develops in his own account as that, whose involvement with nature makes History possible.

Furthermore, Lessing refutes the possibility that historical certainties can lead to faith. The historical is for both, Lessing and Climacus, a relative factor that may not be appropriated infinitely. Lessing states this fact ironically:

> To this I answer: *First*, who will deny (not I) that the reports of these miracles and prophecies are as reliable as historical truths ever can be? But if they are only as reliable as this, why are they treated as if they were infinitely more reliable?... And in what way? In this way, that something quite different and much greater is founded upon them than it is legitimate to found upon truths historically proved...If no historical truth can be demonstrated, then nothing can be demonstrated by means of historical truths.[21]

History should be accepted on the relative ground of finitude. The impossibility of deriving proofs for historical facts cancels out the possibility to consider it as adequate support for accepting the prophecies and miracles of Christ. Lessing's position is comparable to Climacus's view for which History may mislead the passion of faith to appropriate the reporter of the prophecies instead of the teachings of Christ. Lessing asserts his position on the relation of historical proofs and faith in Christ in the following:

> I do not for one moment deny that in Christ prophecies were fulfilled; I do not for one moment deny that Christ performed miracles. But since the truth of these miracles has completely ceased to be demonstrable by miracles still happening at the present time, since they are no more than reports of miracles (however incontroverted and incontrovertible they may be), I deny that they can and should bind me in the least to a faith in the other teachings of Christ. These other teachings I accept on other grounds.[222]

Moreover, Lessing's influence upon Climacus's discussion of the possible relations of the latest generation to the god becomes apparent in Lessing's rejection of granting acceptance to the miracles and teachings of Christ upon syllogistic ground. For both, Lessing and Climacus, the message of Christ eludes logical certainty due to its non-cognitive nature. Lessing thinks that:

> Then *secondly*: What does it mean to accept an historical proposition as true? To believe an historical truth? Does it mean anything other than this: to accept this proposition, this truth as valid? To accept that there is no objection to be brought against it? To accept that one historical proposition is built on one thing, another on another, that from one historical truth another follows? To reserve to oneself the right to estimate other historical things accordingly? Does it mean anything other than this? Anything more? Examine carefully?[223]

Lessing illustrates his view through the very structure of the paragraph, which is formulated in such a way to suggest that a logical relation can only yield numerous propositions. The initial question in the paragraph generates a set of questions in the same manner that the attempt to grasp the instructions of Christ by logical means can only produce a set of propositions.

According to Lesssing, to have faith in Christ as the Son of God is feasible through a different relation. The revelation of God in time or the paradox has to be considered from the perspective of belief in order for its subjective consequences to unfold in the proper domain. "That the Christ, against whose resurrection I can raise no important historical objection, therefore declared himself to be the Son of God; that his disciples therefore believed him to be such; this I gladly believe from my heart. For these truths, as truths of one and the same class, follow quite naturally on one another."[224] In contradistinction to Greek dialectic, Lessing believes that subjective appropriation is feasible through the heart. Faith stands as the ideal *organon* of the Christian experience for both thinkers. The heart is to Lessing what faith and belief are to Climacus. Lessing opposes any association of the historical with faith. He sees them as two extremes that only an arbitrary association can link. On this point Lessing concurs with Climacus's position by not nullifying historical certainty entirely and positing it as the occasion for belief. According to Lessing, to become faithful from the historical standpoint demands a *leap*. It is noteworthy that the *leap* is also a pivotal notion in Kierkegaardian literature. Lessing states that:

> If you press me still further and say: 'Oh yes! This is more than historically certain. For it is asserted by inspired historians who cannot make a mistake.'...But, unfortunately, that also is only historically certain, that these historians were inspired and could not err...That, then, is the ugly broad ditch which I cannot get across, however often and however earnestly I have tried to make the leap. If anyone can help me over it, let him do it, I beg him, I adjure him. He will deserve a reward from me.[125]

Hence, Lessing's *On the Proof of the Spirit and of Power* addresses the same essential aspects of Climacus's project. Climacus's discussion resembles the arguments of Lessing in the context of responding to the question: Whether eternal happiness can be reached from a historical point of departure? In the same manner that only the god may provide the condition for Climacus, Lessing holds that one has to relate to the instructions of Christ independently of any intervention of a third party. Lessing summarizes his view in the following statement:

> But since the truth of these miracles has completely ceased to be demonstrable by miracles still happening now, since they are no more than reports of miracles (even though they be narratives which have not been, and cannot be, impugned), I deny that they can and should bind me to the very least faith in the other teachings of Christ...What then does bind me? Nothing but these teachings themselves.[126]

Conclusion

Climacus's discussion of the relation of the followers at second hand with the god brings the exposition of the *Philosophical Fragments* to an end. The outcome of the investigation that sets out to determine whether the individual's eternal happiness can have a historical starting point is that historical certainty of the existence of the god may serve as the occasion for the individual in each generation to appropriate the god by the means of belief–the organon of faith. The god is resurrected in each generation because the individual's belief is the means through which Christ, as the expression of the eternal, re-enters the historical. Following Climacus's indication to contextualize the above question in its proper domain: "I do not deny this, nor shall I conceal the fact that I did it deliberately and that in the next section of this pamphlet, if I ever do write it, I intend to call the matter by its proper name and clothe the issue in its historical costume.",[227] the following section considers the *Postscript* in which Climacus—after delineating the basic concepts and issues of the *Fragments*—proceeds to deepen his reflections while being sensitive to their historical contextualization.

Climacus's *Concluding Unscientific Postscript*

Approximation and Appropriation

The fact that the *Fragments* concludes with an indirect engagement with Lessing is not accidental. The discussion of the relation of the god with the followers at second hand and its commonality with Lessing's assertion that only individual involvement with the teachings of Christ allows one to believe with the heart draws the continuity of the *Fragments* and *Postscript*. The *Fragments* ends with an implicit elaboration of Lessing's position and the first part of the *Postscript* prepares the ground for Climacus's further reflection on Lessing as the exemplar of the subjective thinker. However, before delving in the subject matter of the *Postscript*, Climacus uses the introduction to elucidate the relation of the *Fragments* and *Postscript*. Climacus describes his satisfaction with the fact that the *Fragments* was not received as a literary thrill; for Climacus, the success of the work consists in its failure to be the center of discussion among the Danish intelligentsia. The *Fragments* is meant to be a literary deception, which by deceiving accomplishes its purpose. Climacus comments on the deceiving nature of the work in the *Introduction*: "As far as my promise is concerned, its casual form was not in the least accidental, because the promise, essentially understood, was no promise, inasmuch as it had been fulfilled in the pamphlet itself. If an issue is divided into an easier part and a more difficult one, the author making the promise ought to proceed by beginning with the easier part and promise the more difficult part as sequel."¹ The *Fragments* is deceptive in the fact that unlike *Either/Or* it was not structured to be praised for its aesthetic virtues in the Danish literary circle. It is thus deliberate that the dense philosophical nature of the *Fragments* renders it impervious to readers with no philosophical and theological training. Climacus strengthens the fundamental role of the *Fragments* in the discussion that it is intended to be read with its companion piece. In the above statement Climacus is asserting that the gist of the issue has been already set up in the *Fragments*; the *Postscript* is going to be a different disguise or its expression in 'historical costume'.

> But it is much more frivolous of him to complete the more difficult part and then to promise a sequel, especially the sort of sequel that any attentive reader of the first part, provided he has the requisite education, can easily write on his own—if he should find it worth the trouble...So it is with *Philosophical Fragments*: the sequel, as mentioned, was only supposed to clothe the issue in historical costume. The issue was the difficulty, that is, if there is anything difficult at all in the whole matter; the historical costume is easy enough.'

Climacus's ironical claim in the above announces the level of difficulty of the *Postscript* and to suggest that it is going to be less convoluted. The relation of the *Fragments* and *Postscript* suggests an ironical presentation. The Irony consists in Climacus's deliberate presentation of the issue under 'historical costume' which is supposed to be easily grasped despite the mammoth size of the *Postscript*. On the other hand, the appearance of the *Fragments*, as the more difficult presentation of the issue, is shorter and seems congenial to readers. Thus it is in accordance with Climacus's ironical presentation of the two texts that the process of developing the notions of the *Fragments* and their implicit aspects is philosophically more taxing and requires a longer exposition. Debunking the key notions of the *Fragments* makes it possible to emphasize the specific junctures of the *Postscript* in which Climacus is elaborating upon the aspects of the issues that have been previously developed. The expression of Climacus's Irony is the enormous appearance of the 'historical costume' of the issue, which suggests difficulty whereas it is really light and easily grasped. On the other hand, the 'small pamphlet'—the *Fragments*—in contradiction to its size articulates the complex categories in theories which provide the gist of the investigation. Climacus requires that the reader be discriminating in reading the *Postscript*. The reader has to try to discern the issues under their 'historical costume', since they are scattered and masked in a larger context. In order to guide the reader in the process, Climacus reiterates the aims of the *Fragments* and its transfiguration in 'historical costume'.

> The issue presented in that pamphlet, yet without the pretense of having solved it, since the pamphlet wanted only to present it, reads as follows: *Can a historical point of departure be given for an eternal consciousness; how can such a point of departure be of more than historical interest; can an eternal happiness be built on historical knowledge?* (see the title page). In the pamphlet itself, the following passage is found: 'As is well known, Christianity is the only historical phenomenon that despite the historical—indeed, precisely by means of the historical—has wanted to be the single individual's point of departure for his eternal consciousness, has wanted to interest him otherwise than merely historically, has wanted to base his happiness on his relation to something historical.' Thus, in historical costume, the issue in question is Christianity. Accordingly, the issue pertains to Christianity. In treatise form, the issue could be formulated less problematically this way: the apologetical presuppositions of faith, approximational transition and overtures to faith, the quantifying introduction to the decision of faith.'

However, Climacus warns us that the goal of the *Postscript* is not to give an objective account of Christianity. The historical reflections on Christianity are not going to thematize its origin and development along various historical periods. Rather, Climacus wishes to elaborate the ethos of the ideal Christian way of life; the way that each follower comes to receive the condition from the god. Climacus's aim is to develop how subjectivity appropriates Christianity passionately and independently of any objectivity. "In order, however, to avoid confusion, it should immediately be borne in mind that the issue is not about the truth of Christianity but about the individual's relation to Christianity, consequently not about the indifferent individual's systematic eagerness to arrange the truths of Christianity in paragraphs but rather about the concern of the infinitely interested individual with regard to his own relation to such a doctrine."' Hence the various categories that Climacus develops theoretically and independently of social and historical relations in the *Fragments* are going to assume their historical application in the self's subjective relation to eternal happiness. The follower, historically considered, is the self and the god is the one who gives the condition to achieve the essentially Christian. Moreover, Climacus is aware of the implication of dealing with the issue in 'historical costume' because, according to him, to consider the relation of the self to eternal happiness implies the acknowledgment of the objectification of the question. The objective reception of the issue needs to be considered as well for the project to be complete. It is in response to this necessity that Climacus asserts that the clarification of the issue requires both, an objective and subjective treatments. He states that: "In order to make my issue as clear as possible, I shall first present the objective issue and show how that is treated. The historical will thereby receive its due. Next, I shall present the subjective issue...The first part is the promised sequel; the second part is a renewed attempt in the same vein as the pamphlet, a new approach to the issue of *Fragments*."[5] It is noteworthy that Climacus ascribes a circular infrastructure to the project by starting with the *Fragments* and then the *Postscript* in order to return to the theme of the former in a novel fashion.

In the first part of the *Postscript,* Climacus focuses on the dominant ways that one can relate to Christianity objectively. Climacus follows the inherent constituents of each historical relation in order to point out their unsuitability. Under the objective light, Christianity may be grasped in two ways: historically and philosophically. The objectification of Christianity opens up History and Philosophy as the two socio-cultural media that Climacus must assess. In Climacus's words: "Thus, objectively understood, truth can signify: (1) historical truth, (2) philosophical truth. Viewed as historical truth, the truth must be established by a critical consideration of the various reports etc., in short, in the same way as historical truth is ordinarily established. In the case of philosophical truth, the inquiry turns on the relation of a doctrine, historically given and verified, to the eternal truth."[6] The limitation of the objective relation is that it functions according to a disinterested attitude in which the person accepts the authority of the Christian media. The disinterested attitude reinforces the dominant role of the Bible and the Church as the traditional Christian instruments. The Holy Scripture and Church stand as the primary means to verify the authenticity of Christianity for the *relationship of observation*. The Church represents the contemporary source of authority for the disinterested person to relate to Christianity. Climacus develops the dynamics of the Holy Scripture and the Church to deconstruct their contribution to the objective relation to Christianity.

The objective view of Christianity inevitably ascribes it the status of a natural science. Its scientific nature, from the objective attitude, derives from the fact that it has to undergo the usual process of investigation and verification of the natural sciences. Climacus posits the Bible as the central medium for this process because it is the bearer of the data that are traditionally called upon to support the veracity of Christianity. Climacus's endeavor is aware of the tendency of his contemporaries because as Westphal remarks: "In the nineteenth century both, History and Philosophy claimed to be scientific, not because they imitated the experimental and quantitative methods of the natural sciences but because they developed methods that enabled them to achieve the same sort of disinterested objectivity, free from personal bias or communal ideology."[7] It is in response to this prevailing inclination that Climacus thinks that: "If Christianity is viewed as a historical document, the important thing is to obtain a completely reliable report of what the Christian doctrine really is...When the truth of Christianity is asked about historically, or what is and what is not Christian truth, Holy Scripture immediately presents itself as a crucial document. Therefore, the historical point of view focuses first on the Bible."[8] To undermine the scientific expectation that the disinterested person holds from Christianity, Climacus shows the inherent flaw in the objective interpretation of the Bible. Climacus comments on the undeniable scholarship that is involved in the critical evaluation of the various books of the Bible, since their genuineness strengthens Christianity for the disinterested person. "Here the canonicity of particular books is dealt with, their authenticity and integrity, the author's axiopisty, and a dogmatic guarantee is posited: inspiration."[9] However, the conscientiousness of the investigation of the Biblical texts cannot result in the subjective appropriation of Christianity. For Climacus, it is a scholarly mishap to expect inspiration from the critical and academic investigation of the texts of the Holy Scriptures; subjective inspiration is elusive to critical analysis. Climacus thinks that subjective inspiration can emerge only from the investment of faith in the words of the prophet and not from the cognitive faculties' analysis of the Bible. "The misrelation between inspiration and critical research is like that between eternal happiness and critical deliberations, because inspiration is an object only for faith."[10]

In addition, the scientific attitude encounters an insuperable obstacle. Climacus observes that the collection of data and their assessment result in a piecemeal account of Christianity. Unlike the object of scientific investigation, Christianity is essentially elusive to sensory perceptions. Thus, the cognitive process is involved in a self-defeating endeavor by trying to conceptualize the genuineness of Christianity. Climacus denounces the futility of objectifying the Bible in the following: "It must then be that this objectivity and this modesty were out of place, were un-Christian. Then it certainly would be dubious to enter the truth of Christianity in this manner. Christianity is spirit; spirit is inwardness; inwardness is subjectivity; subjectivity is essentially passion, and at its maximum an infinite, personally interested passion for one's eternal happiness."[11] The academic theologian and objective observer can only infer on the basis of the existing relations among the books of the Bible, but cannot—subjectively by the means of faith—be inspired by them.

The Church confronts the same difficulty when it is posited as an authority to support Christianity in the socio-cultural domain. Climacus is referring to the Danish Church as the predominant Christian institution in Protestant Denmark.

Moreover, the Bible is the basis of the Church which in turn makes it feasible to approach Christianity scientifically. "But also within Protestantism, after the Bible has been abandoned as a secure stronghold, there has been recourse to the Church."[12] Climacus's assessment of the role of the Church is in order because it constitutes the prevailing source of Christian authority in his socio-cultural setting. He acknowledges it in the claim that: "Turning the matter so as to relinquish the Bible and resort to the Church is indeed a Danish idea."[13] The Church, like the Bible, has to be inspiring to fulfill its Christian mission. Thus, critical academic investigation of the Church can only result in data gathering and idle chatter among scholars. On the basis of the above discussion, Climacus introduces a central term to express the inadequacy of the objectification of Christianity by historical means, mainly: *approximation.*

Climacus is here delineating an important theme of Kierkegaardian literature. Approximation represents the limitation of the objective undertakings because the subject matter of History is always absent to sensory perceptions. It is primarily because of the approximation that is inherent to History that Climacus regards it as misleading to relate absolutely to History. It forces the inquirer in a logical relation with the Church and the Bible in which she climbs from one premise to the other while being only certain of the initial premise. It is because of the illusory outcome of this process that Climacus makes this claim about the Bible, which is also pertinent to the Church:

> The first dialectical difficulty with the Bible is that it is a historical document, that as soon as it is made the stronghold an introductory approximation commences, and the subject is divested into a parenthesis, the conclusion of which one awaits for all Eternity. The New Testament is something of the past and is thus historical in a stricter sense. This is the beguiling aspect that prevents making the issue subjective and treats it objectively, whereby it never comes into existence at all. – *Philosophical Fragments* focuses on this difficulty in chapters 4 and 5 by canceling the difference between the contemporary follower and the latest follower, who are presumed to be separated by 1800 years.[14]

Climacus's reference to chapters 4 and 5 of the *Fragments* is meant to show that the objectification of Christianity via historical means shares the same difficulty with the followers' attempt to relate to the god through historical reports of trustworthy sources. The objectification of Christianity by the means of the Bible and the Church runs the same risk of misleading the passion of faith by basing it upon History. The approximation of the historical is then another expression of the fruitless logical relation to the existence of the god, since Christianity is intrinsically paradoxical.

Climacus thinks that the approximation and the misuse of faith that absolutize the historical is an escape mechanism through which the objective inquirer avoids the call to take the leap of faith. Taking the leap of faith consists in accepting the distress and uncertainty of becoming a Christian. The objectification of Christianity is thus the failure to assume responsibility in the face of the absolute *Other*; it is the refusal to allow the essentially Christian to structure the self's subjectivity. "The eighteen centuries are indeed supposed to instill terror. As a demonstration *pro*, they = 0 for the individual subject in the moment of decision, but as a terror *contra*, they are superb."[15] Climacus deliberately includes the 'moment' of decision in order to allude to his previous discussion of the *moment* in the *Fragments*. The moment that separates the Greek period and the rise Christianity is constitutive for subjective's self-transcendence. Climacus is asserting here the need for the self to become responsible toward the infinite *Other*.

The philosophical outlook on Christianity bears scientific expectations, as well. Their objectification of Christianity is not as obvious as that of the theologians because their critical evaluation is not based upon the scrutiny of the Biblical texts and the Church. Climacus believes that the speculative approach to Christianity strives to suffuse it with thought in order to raise it to the status of an eternal idea. Speculative Philosophy wishes to eternalize Christianity by historicizing it. Climacus thinks that: "The speculative point of view conceives of Christianity as a historical phenomenon; the question of its truth therefore becomes a matter of permeating it with thought in such a way that finally Christianity itself is the eternal thought."[16] Climacus's concern is that speculative Philosophy reduces Christianity to a mere object of contemplation and deprives it of its transformative power for the self. It neutralizes Christianity because for the speculative observer, "It is a matter of indifference to him whether or not anyone accepts it;"[17]

In addition, Climacus thinks that to philosophize about Christianity is useless because it erroneously presupposes that Christianity is immediately accessible. Thus, both, speculative Philosophy and the critical assessment of the Bible and the Church are susceptible to this error. Climacus points out the flaw in the philosophical rationalization of Christianity by drawing out the role of belief in the process. The absolute certainty that the philosophical undertaking claims to achieve is indeed illusory because the philosopher can genuinely relate to Christianity only by the means of belief. To stress this fact, Climacus refers to his previous discussion of the role of belief in positing the historical in the *Fragments*: "The speculative thinker looks at Christianity as a historical phenomenon...If a speculative thinker were to say that he had comprehended the necessity of a historical phenomenon, I would indeed bid him to occupy himself for a moment with the misgivings set forth in all simplicity in the Interlude between chapters 4 and 5 of the *Fragments*."[18] To recall the discussion in the *Fragments*, Climacus shows that the fact that the historical is never immediately accessible requires that the uncertainty that derives from its absence be negated. Consequently, it is essential to the act of believing to overcome uncertainty by accepting precisely what it cannot experience immediately. "This is precisely the nature of belief [*Tro*], for continually present as the nullified in the certitude of belief is the incertitude that in every way corresponds to the uncertainty of coming into existence. Thus, belief believes what it does not see;"[19] Climacus exposes the contradiction in elevating Christianity to an eternal idea because the very point of departure—belief—is in conflict with the absolute certainty that the speculative philosopher is seeking.

After demonstrating the futile role of History and the centuries that separate the various generations from the existence of the god in objectifying Christianity, Climacus shifts his focus to another frequent misappropriation. As an extension of the attempt to objectify Christianity, the comic relation to Christianity occurs when someone absolutizes the speculative relation to Christianity in a passionate manner. This misrelation happens at the apex of the philosophical rationalization of Christianity because it presupposes that the speculative philosopher has previously developed the numerous steps of a method to objectify Christianity. Consequently, the speculative philosopher regards such accomplishment as eternal. For Climacus, the indifference of the speculative thinker toward Christianity is dogmatic, since she does not seek to secure eternal happiness on the ground of what has been accomplished, but merely posits it as an object of contemplation.

> Or the speculative thinker is not a believer. The speculator, of course, is not comic, for he does not at all ask about his eternal happiness. The comic first emerges when the impassioned, infinitely interested subjective individual wants to relate his happiness to speculative thought. But the speculative thinker does not raise the issue we are discussing, because as a speculative thinker he becomes precisely too objective to concern himself with his eternal happiness.[20]

This misappropriation is reminding of Climacus's previous example of the tyrant in the *Fragments*, who as a member of the first generation of the followers at second hand, strives passionately to establish the existence of the god by the means of meticulous investigation of historical reports. The misuse of faith that is based on historical data derives from the similar disposition as the comic attitude, which is grounded on speculative Philosophy. Climacus develops the notion of the

comic as a counterpart of approximation as the main theme of his discussion of the objectification of Christianity.
Paradigm of the Subjective

Climacus's account of the objective version of the issue is scarce in comparison to the substantial discussion of Christianity from the subjective perspective. The brevity of the objective section suggests that Climacus either holds little esteem for the objective perspective or that he sets it up as a mere foil on the basis of which the subjective position is to thrive. However, the first option does not hold because Climacus consistently refers to the thesis of the objectification of Christianity in the rest of the *CUP*. Hence the fact that Climacus deliberately positions the objective issue at the beginning of the text and its briefness has structural purpose. Another significant aspect of the composition of the subjective discussion is that, unlike the objective one, Climacus does not start his account immediately, but instead introduces his view of Gotthold Lessing. Given the strategic nature of Climacus's style, it is reasonable to wonder about his implicit intention in providing a laudatory summary of Lessing as an author and thinker. Climacus's direct address and praise of Lessing, at this juncture, are surprising and puzzling because they are at variance with his usual critical and subversive attitude toward his predecessors and contemporaries.

Furthermore, Climacus asserts boldly that he is not interested in Lessing's sophistication and scholarly accomplishments. Thus, it is clear that Climacus is not setting out to formulate a formal philosophical attack on Lessing as he has been doing with Hegel and Kant. Climacus is interested in the aspects of Lessing that have eluded the academic and intellectual analysis of his works. Climacus is concerned with the aspects of Lessing's achievements that are beyond formal and academic interpretation. This fact becomes obvious in the following claim:

> The expression of gratitude does not pertain to what is generally and, as I assume, also rightly admired about Lessing. I do not consider myself justified in admiring in that way. My expression does not pertain to Lessing in the capacity of a savant, or to what appeals to me as an ingenious myth, that he was a librarian, or to what appeals to me as an epigram, that he was the soul in a library, that with an almost ubiquitous autopsy he possessed an enormous body of knowledge,"

Climacus thus announces that he is not grateful for the objective part of Lessing's accomplishments. He is interested in Lessing as the embodiment of a unique individuality that no historical summary or 'epigram' can capture. "Climacus broadens the essence of the historical Lessing into universal application by abstracting the supra-individual from the actual individual."²² Climacus considers Lessing as a paradigm because Lessing deliberately preserves his individuality over the formal and historical. It is this conscious achievement that qualifies Lessing as the prototype of the subjective and religious. Climacus "makes the historical Lessing into a pseudonym in order to read him as he (Climacus) and others, including Kierkegaard, suggest reading the pseudonymous literature."²³ Thus, for Climacus, Lessing is assuming the role of a fictitious author whose persona is used to delineate a specific set of qualities. Climacus refutes the objective and historical role of Lessing in order to do away with their quantitative suggestion. Climacus states the cause of his veneration for Lessing in the following:

> No, it pertains to something in which the knotty difficulty is precisely that one cannot come to admire him directly or by one's admiration enter into an immediate relation to him, for his merit consists precisely in having prevented this: he closed himself off in the isolation of subjectivity, did not allow himself to be tricked into becoming world-historical or systematic with regard to the religious, but he understood, and knew how to maintain, that the religious pertained to Lessing and Lessing alone.²⁴

Lessing is the model of the subjective and religious individual because of his mechanism of resistance to objectification. Climacus believes that Lessing had a keen awareness of his individuality and his solitary responsibility before the infinite *Other*.

Climacus is indifferent to the fact that Lessing has published numerous pamphlets and their impact upon his contemporaries. Climacus is accentuating the untold aspect that underlies the polemic religious essays and plays of Lessing. Moreover, Climacus does not emphasize the dominant objective sense that permeates Lessing's writings. Rather, Climacus wants to draw out what he deems to be the religious intensity of Lessing's personality.

> With regard to the religious, he always kept something to himself, something that he certainly did say but in a crafty way, something that could not be reeled off by tutors, something that continually remained the same while it continually changed form, something that was not distributed stereotyped for entry in a systematic formula book, but something that a gymnastic dialectician produces and alters and produces, the same and yet not the same.²⁵

Climacus regards Lessing's works as a series of manifestations of the constant religious intensity that Lessing held within. It is in virtue of his subjective religious devotion that Lessing is reminding of a Kierkegaardian pseudonym that incarnates the topic under consideration.

Lessing reveals much independently of and precisely by the means of the scholarly texts. Climacus's emphasis upon the non-scholarly aspect of Lessing's writings opens up a new approach to his texts. The subjective approach has yet another implication because the subjective message of Lessing requires a subjective disposition on the part of the reader. Climacus refers to Lessing's concealed way to pass on the religious dimension as *indirect communication*. Climacus is emphatic on the fact that Lessing invites the reader to approach his works in a non-systematic way. Indirect communication is indeed the expression of Irony—a feature that Climacus shares with Lessing. What Climacus thinks is meritorious in Lessing's approach is that "Lessing's style as a thinker is Lessing's Irony. He does not instruct the reader or build a system of thought, Johannes Climacus points out, but rather Socratically invites self-reflection by means of polemic and wit. His writings, in the form of the brief essay and aphorism, maintain the pitch of indirection that contributes to such self-reflection."[26] The style of Lessing's writing has the virtue of inciting the reader to self-reflection precisely at the juncture when she sets out to reflect on Lessing. Since, Climacus holds that Lessing has managed to remain elusive through his writings, thus any attempt to appropriate his works can only occasion an inward turn on the part of the reader. Climacus observes about Lessing that: "Truly, no father confessor who received a secret to be kept, no maiden who had pledged herself and her love to silence and became immortal by keeping her pledge, no one who took every piece of information with him into the grave—no one could act more carefully than Lessing in the more difficult task: also to speak. Not even Satan himself is able, as a third party, to say anything with definiteness as a third party."[27] Indirect communication is thus an invitation to the reader to relate to oneself. The element of deception that is involved in this procedure is indeed similar to Socratic teaching. It is *maieutic* to the extent that both, Socrates and Lessing remain deliberately opaque individualities, which always turns the reader inward whenever she tries to relate to them historically and objectively. Hence, Westphal observes correctly that: "Lessing 'teaches' Climacus about subjectivity as Socrates 'teaches' the slave boy in the *Meno* a version of the Pythagorean theorem."[28]

Lessing, in pseudonymous costume, represents the exemplar of the ideal subjective thinker for Climacus. Climacus begins the section on subjectivity with a praise of Lessing in order to assert him as the exemplar of genuine subjectivity. The Lessing that Climacus delineates is the direct contraposition of the speculative thinker who is commensurate with his philosophical writings. To the contrary,

Lessing appropriates Christianity subjectively and manifests it—by the means of his ironic writings—as a relation that each individual is to enter alone with the infinite *Other*. It is in virtue of this fact that Climacus believes Lessing to be the ideal antithesis of Hegel, whom he thinks to be commensurable with his philosophical writings. Hegel is not artistic in his speculative approach because there is nothing excessive in the relation of his individuality to his speculative account of Christianity. Climacus contrasts Lessing and Hegel in the following statement:

> Similarly Hegel also is supposed to have died with the words that no one understood him except one person, who misunderstood him, and if Hegel has done the same thing, it perhaps could serve Lessing for good. But alas, there was quite a difference. In the first place, Hegel's statement has the flaw that it is a direct statement and thus is totally inadequate for such a misunderstanding, and this insufficiently shows that Hegel did not exist artistically in the illusiveness of double-reflection. Next it has the flaw that Hegel's communication in the seventeen whole volumes is direct communication, so that if he has not found anyone who has understood him, it is all the worse for Hegel.[29]

Hegel's speculative Philosophy is strictly literal. The understanding of Hegel's Philosophy does not enrich the self subjectively because it does not occasion any transformation. Furthermore, since Hegel communicated directly, the distortion of his works cannot be of assistance to the self because the distortion only suppresses the direct message and does not provoke subjective change.

On the other hand, Lessing represents the expression of the critique of the objectification of Christianity. Climacus proceeds shrewdly to associate the characteristics of the subjective approach to Christianity with the characterization of Gotthold Lessing as a pseudonymous character. To be effective, Climacus jettisons all the objective and historical constituents of Lessing and draws him as the possessor of the subjective qualities that the religious and subjective individual ought to have. Another accomplishment of Climacus is the introduction of the notion of *appropriation* that is illustrated in Lessing. *Appropriation* is the direct opposite of *approximation*. "Climacus develops the contrast in terms of dialectical tension between *approximation* and *appropriation*."[30] The category of appropriation, unlike approximation, presupposes the individual's subjective relation to the task of being a Christian. By appropriating Christianity, the self accepts the condition of the god to become a genuine Christian.

Lessing's Theses as Subjective Ideals

Climacus manages meticulously to describe Lessing as the embodiment of the subjective ways of life that the individual should emulate in order to become a subjective thinker in chapter one. Lessing's non-historical and indirect message is an invitation to every reader to turn inward in order to deepen subjectivity. By the same token, Climacus employs the brief introduction to Lessing to criticize the limitations of the objective approach to Christianity and to illustrate the proper way one should appropriate the Christian way of life. In the following chapter, *Possible and Actual Theses by Lessing,* Climacus is going to expand the creed of the subjective ways of life for which Lessing stands as the paragon. The theses that Climacus assigns to Lessing constitute the fundamentals of religious subjectivity and expand his account of the fictitious Lessing. Climacus's goal is thus twofold. As a pseudonym himself, Climacus is—in the remainder of the text—going to delineate another pseudonym. The structure of this section is peculiar because Climacus as the pseudonymous author is engaged into delineating Lessing as another fictitious character.

The structure of the subjective discussion of Christianity presents a pseudonym in the process of developing an ideal pseudonym, while establishing the essentials of subjectivity and religious experience. Climacus declares his intention in a hesitant fashion in the following:

> I now intend to present something that I shall, what the deuce, ascribe to Lessing, without being certain that he would acknowledge it, something that I in teasing exuberance could easily be tempted to want to foist upon him as something he said, although not directly, something for which in a different sense I in admiration could enthusiastically wish to dare to thank him, something that in turn I ascribe to him with proud restraint and self-esteem, just out of generosity, and then again something that I fear will offend or bother him by linking his name to it.[31]

Thus, according to Climacus's strategy, the ideal Lessing and the ideal subjectivity are both, in the process of definition. Unlike the historical Lessing, the ideal Lessing will take shape simultaneously as the development of the proper ways to be subjective. "the Lessing figure in the *Postscript* is presented as the embodiment of the subjectively existing thinker who insures himself against fellowship and prevents discipleship."[32] Climacus is now in the position to undertake his task because the subjective ways of life and Lessing have been demarcated by being contrasted with the objective standpoint. Hence, the preliminary discussion of the objective reception of Christianity was meant to point out the opposite of the subjective life and to prepare the reader for the ideals of Lessing.

The first thesis that Climacus ascribes to Lessing is that: "*The subjective thinker is aware of the dialectic of communication.*"[33] Through this thesis, Climacus provides a fresh definition of the act of communication. The dialectic of communication that Climacus is positing is indeed a deepening of the usual way of communication. In indirect communication, the interlocutor is involved in the process of transmitting the idea, while being concerned about the expression of her subjective life in the idea. To communicate indirectly requires that there is syncretism between the communicator's existence and the idea that is being passed on to the other. "Whereas objective thinking is indifferent to the thinking subject and his existence, the subjective thinker as existing is essentially interested in his own thinking, is existing in it."[34] The dynamics of indirect communication is, in addition, the invitation to one's interlocutor to carry out the same subjective dialectic. The objective relation that takes place in the event of indirect communication is only apparent. Each party, by the means of speech, as the universal mode of communication, takes the inward turn toward subjectivity. The indirect communicators are *maieutic* to one another in that they create the bridge between the other and her inwardness. "The reflection of inwardness is the subjective thinker's double-reflection. In thinking, he thinks the universal, but, as existing in this thinking, as acquiring this in his inwardness, he becomes more and more subjectively isolated."[35] Although, 'being subjectively isolated' may suggest that indirect communication generates a melancholic disposition, the experience of isolation is a necessary stage in the individual's preparation to stand alone in the religious relation.

For Climacus, the transformation of the usual means of communication alters the content as well. The transmission of the truth that is carried out by direct communication no longer holds; the truth cannot be sought in the configuration of the words, which remain merely universal. The particular transmission of the truth lies in the way that the truth is communicated. Climacus is emphatic on the fact that: "objectively there is no truth, but the appropriation is the truth...The main point was indeed to become understood, and the inwardness of the understanding would indeed be that the single individual would understand this by himself."[36] Climacus's position shows sensitiveness to the individual's autonomy as a communicator. The communicator's autonomy consists in the fact that the individual no longer needs to accept the idea as it is handed out objectively, but must develop the ability to appropriate it in the manner that suits her subjective situation.

It is in virtue of the autonomy of indirect communication that Climacus posits it as an art form. Every act of indirect communication stands on its own independently of any objective association and waits to be appropriated on subjective terms. Acts of indirect communication are comparable to works of art that lead every communicator inward. Climacus thinks that: "Wherever the subjective is of importance in knowledge and appropriation is therefore the main point, communication is a work of art; it is doubly reflected, and its first form is the subtlety that the subjective individuals must be held devoutly apart from one another and must not run coagulatingly together in objectivity. This is objectivity's word of farewell to subjectivity."[37] The individual's commitment to indirect communication is the inevitable renunciation of the implicit tyranny of objective language. Climacus links the freedom that derives from indirect communication with the motif of the secret. "just as the subjective existing thinker has set himself free by the duplexity, so the secret of communication specifically hinges on setting the other free."[38] The theme of the secret has profound implications. It is the secrecy of subjectivity that is involved in the religious relation—the secrecy of inwardness. The secrecy, that indirect communication occasions, is essentially the ineffability that occurs when one attempts or is forced to communicate objectively the excess of the religious experience. The excess of the religious relation is the aspect that cannot be verbally expressed; it can only be lived. Climacus idealizes Lessing because despite his writings on religious issues, he manages to preserve the secret. "Lessing himself remained silent through speaking. What he said is independent of *his* actuality and has to be so if what he says is to be communicated adequately to another."[39] Climacus elaborates the notion of the secret further:

> Ordinary communication, objective thinking, has no secrets; only doubly reflected subjective thinking has secrets; that is, all its essential content is essentially a secret, because it cannot be communicated directly. This is the significance of the secrecy. That this knowledge cannot be stated directly, because the essential in this knowledge is the appropriation itself, means that it remains a secret for everyone who is not through himself doubly reflected in the same way, but that this is the essential form of truth means that this cannot be said in any other way.[40]

The secret dwells in the excess of the religious relation. Climacus presents the subjective thinker as an artist who in the isolation of subjectivity intensifies the secret of the religious experience. Climacus contrasts the secret of inwardness, as the essential secret, with the accidental secret. The accidental secret derives from objective procedures that happen in social or political settings. "For example what has been said in a privy council is an accidental secret as long as it is not publicly known, because the statement itself can be understood directly as soon as it is made public."⁴¹ The essential feature of the accidental secret is that it agrees with the objective expectation of society. On the other hand, the essential secret of the religious relation cannot be understood by the public, which regards it as an absurd expression. "Everything subjective, which on account of its dialectical inwardness evades the direct form of expression, is an essential secret."⁴²

The second thesis is an illustration of the *existence-relation*. For Climacus, this relation is defined by the self's continuous attempt to become subjective. Existence is not a determined state of being. It is positive because it is involved in the process of becoming and also negative since it is never a fixed state. "*In his existence-relation to the truth, the existing subjective thinker is just as negative as positive, has just as much of the comic as he essentially has of pathos, and is continually in the process of becoming, that is, striving*."⁴³ The subjective thinker has the privilege of double reflection. Climacus thinks that the consciousness that existence is never determinate belongs only to the subjective thinker. It is the consciousness of this negative state that represents the positive. "The negative thinkers therefore always have the advantage that they have something positive, namely this, that they are aware of the negative; the positive thinkers have nothing whatever, for they are deluded."⁴⁴ The delusion of the positive thinkers is the belief that they have a hold over existence, which is continually in flux. The negative thinker avoids being deceived by accepting that existence is by nature transitory.

The awareness of the dual aspect of existence yields its pathetic and comic sides. For Climacus the pathos of existence is the fact that it is a never-ending pursuit that aims at reaching the infinite. It is also comic because of the inherent contradiction of the process; to strive toward the infinite that is unreachable is indeed a comic endeavor. "Existence itself, existing is a striving and is just as pathos-filled as it is comic: pathos-filled because the striving is infinite, that is, directed toward the infinite, is a process of infinitizing, which is the highest pathos; comic because the striving is a self-contradiction."⁴⁵ The negative thinker—by being aware of the dual aspect of existence—achieves both, the finite and infinite sides of existence. Thus, the subjective thinker's attitude agrees with the dual outcome of the coming of the god, which is the expression of the eternal in the historical as finite. "But what is existence? It is that child who is begotten by the infinite and the finite, the eternal and the temporal, and is therefore continually striving."⁴⁶ It is in virtue of this realization that the subjective thinker has the infinite within her.

The following thesis pertains to the discussion of the *Fragments* in alluding to the question: Whether eternal happiness is achievable through historical knowledge? Climacus relies on Lessing's thesis because it introduces the notion of the leap as the appropriate means. "*Lessing has said that contingent historical truths can never become a demonstration of eternal truths of reason, also that the transition whereby one will build an eternal truth on historical reports is a leap.*"[47] Climacus applies Lessing's thesis in the Christian context of eternal happiness. Hence, Climacus assigns the notion of the leap to Christianity, which is the sole avenue through which eternal happiness is achievable. "The basis of the paradox of Christianity is that it continually uses time and the historical in relation to the eternal."[48] The legitimate ground of Climacus's application of the notion of the leap in a different context than that of Lessing is that he regards it as the "category of decision"[49] In both, contexts, the individual carries the transition through inwardness. Christianity demands inward transformation and resists every quantitative acceptance—biblical or through the Church. Climacus believes that "Lessing perceives very well that the leap, as decisive, is qualitatively dialectical and permits no approximating transition."[50] In the Kierkegaardian corpus, the best illustration of the qualitative leap in the Christian context is the character of Abraham—the knight of faith. Abraham is the ideal subject who undertakes the leap from the finite to the infinite. Climacus expresses this fact in the allusion to *Fear and Trembling*: "Before getting a chance to read that volume by Lessing, I had read *Fear and Trembling* by Johannes de Silentio. In that book I had perceived how the leap, according to the author, as the decision χατ' ἐξοχην [par excellence] becomes specifically decisive for what is Christian and for every dogmatic category."[51] The example of Abraham represents the assurance that the application of Lessing's notion of the leap is applicable to Climacus's discussion of Christianity as well.

The fourth thesis of Lessing epitomizes the notion of striving that Climacus associates with the existence-relation. The thesis is a statement in, which Lessing refutes the possibility of achieving truth in favor of striving toward it. "[If God held all enclosed truth in his right hand, and in his left hand the one and only ever-striving drive for truth, even with the corollary of erring forever and ever, and if he were to say to me: Choose!—I would humbly fall down to him at his left hand and say: Father, give! Pure truth is indeed only for you alone]!"[52] In these words, Lessing exemplifies the negative thinker's awareness that the truth is never fixed, and that it is a continuous process of striving the same way that Climacus previously asserts that existence is pathos-filled through its continuous nature. Climacus believes that Lessing's confession to be more meritorious than the systematician's because it confesses impotence and does not pretend to establish a definite system. "So these two, Lessing and the systematician, both, speak of a continued striving—the only difference is that Lessing is obtuse or truthful enough too call it a continued striving, the systematician sagacious or untruthful enough to call it the system."⁵³ Subjective existence is thus elusive to systematic grasp. Climacus concludes, on the basis of its striving aspect, that a system of existence cannot be given, whereas, a logical system can be given. Climacus reaches these conclusions because "It is the temporality of the thinker's existence that makes totality and system impossible, and that in turn makes the claim to a finished existence comical."⁵⁴

The possibility of a logical system depends upon the exclusion of any aspect of subjective existence. Climacus thinks that the essential characteristic of the logical system is the omission of every existential consideration. "In a logical system, nothing may be incorporated that has a relation to existence, that is not indifferent to existence."⁵⁵ The system thrives essentially upon the negative relation to subjective existence. Climacus stresses the conceptual nature of the logical system by showing that it starts with abstraction from the immediate. "The beginning of the system that begins with the immediate *is then itself achieved through reflection.*"⁵⁶ The logical system is essentially antithetical to the existence-relation.

The system of existence is inconceivable because of the oxymoronic relation of system and existence. For Climacus, the indifference of the system toward every existential aspect makes it absurd to think existence and system together. In addition, the system presupposes a fixed point of culmination, whereas, existence is essentially a never-ending striving. "System and conclusiveness correspond to each other, but existence is the very opposite. Abstractly viewed, system and existence cannot be thought conjointly, because in order to think existence, systematic thought must think it as annulled and consequently as not existing."⁵⁷ To posit the possibility of the system of existence is indeed presumptuous and even unethical, for Climacus. Given that existence is never conclusive from the human standpoint and that only God enjoys the privilege of grasping the totality of existence, the systematician of existence is thus engaged in playing God. "Whereas thought and being are interchangeable for Hegel, who wished to see things from a divine vantage point, Kierkegaard stresses the view that, for man, thought and being are not identical. To think about Christianity is something completely different from being a Christian."⁵⁸ Conflating system and existence or thinking about Christianity and being a Christian is immoral because it is offensive to divine will. "It follows that such a thinker must be either the good Lord or a fantastical *quodlibet* [anything]. Certainly everyone will perceive the immorality in this, and certainly everyone will also perceive that what another author has observed regarding the Hegelian system is entirely in order: that through Hegel a system, the absolute system, was brought to completion—without having an ethics."⁵⁹ Climacus thinks that Hegel—by developing the system—wishes to play God. Climacus concludes his elaboration of the theses of Lessing with a metaphor. The attempt of the subjective thinker to reconcile her eternal happiness with the historical is feasible because the leap is essentially an effort that can be carried out within the finite situation of the temporal. On the other hand, to want to set up a system of existence is comparable to the act of flying, which lies beyond the abilities of every human being.

The Passion of Faith and the Subjective Thinker

Climacus starts this section by asserting an important aspect of the discussion of subjectivity. The distinctive mark of the issue of subjectivity is that it is the delineation of the issue of subjectivity itself. In contrast to other issues that can be discussed from an objective perspective, which allows one to remain indifferent, subjectivity is essentially *the issue*. Subjectivity becomes an issue within the self for whom it is problematic. The problem of subjectivity is never extrinsic to the inner life of the one who contemplates it. "It must continually be insisted upon that the subjective issue is not something about the case in point but is the subjectivity itself."⁶⁰ The discussion of subjectivity, as an issue, calls upon the subject to make the decision to become subjective. To approach it otherwise is, for Climacus, to avoid the inner distress and responsibility of making the decision.

Another significant aspect of the second section of the *CUP* is that Climacus associates the possibility of subjectivity with genuine Christianity. The subjective thinker is thus on the quest to becoming an authentic Christian. "This development or remaking of the subjectivity, its infinite concentration in itself under a conception of the infinite's highest good, an eternal happiness, is the developed possibility of the subjectivity's first possibility. Christianity, therefore, protests against all objectivity; it wants the subject to be infinitely concerned about himself."⁶¹ Climacus is going to develop the ethos of subjectivity in agreement with the ideals of genuine Christianity. This fact is fundamental to understand the dual structure of the text, which are its religious and philosophical aims. Moreover, Climacus does not address these two aspects only from the theoretical perspective, but presents Lessing as their concrete expression.

Subjectivity and Christianity are linked through faith as their defining characteristic. Climacus contrasts faith, as the transfiguring power of inwardness, with the ethical that assures the individual's success in social contexts. That the ethical—the acceptance of social norms as absolute—is in opposition to faith becomes obvious in Climacus's parenthetical claim that: "(To be an observer, that is the ethical! That a person ought to be an observer is the *ethical* answer—)"[62] The ethical attitude confines the self to the events of the external world; the ethical individuality is committed strictly to the ethical norms of her social context. It is in agreement with this position that Climacus sets out to argue the inadequacy of the ethical in the face of Christianity and subjectivity. "so I, too, shall now pause with a few introductory observations regarding the objective orientation: *what ethics would have to judge if becoming a subjective individual were not the highest task assigned to every human being.*"[63] Climacus believes that the ethical is subjectively impotent; it is unsuitable to bring about subjective transformations in the self. The ethical is effective only within the domain of finitude, which is always beyond the social agent's control. "A truly great ethical individuality would consummate his life as follows: he would develop himself to the utmost of his capability; in the process he perhaps would produce a great effect in the external world, but this would not occupy him at all, because he would know that the external is not in his power and therefore means nothing either *pro* or contra."[64] Climacus thinks that the ethical, being rewarding in the finite world, may stand between the self and God. The individual runs the risk of absolutizing the ethical instead of God. "He does not want to understand that there is nothing between him and God but the ethical; he does not want to understand that he ought to be made enthusiastic by it; he does not want to understand that God, without doing any injustice and without denying his nature, which is love, could create a human being endowed with capacities unmatched by all others,"[65] In the Kierkegaardian corpus, the ethical individuality finds expression in Judge William who apotheosizes the ethical. On the other hand, the transcendence of the ethical is illustrated in Abraham's obedience to the divine injunction.

The extreme expression of the ethical life is the world-historical. The world-historical is the summit of the observer's attitude; the world-historical individual remains indifferent toward both, the events of the world and subjectivity. As a systematician, the world-historical individuality believes that every historical moment falls within the predicted period that was assigned to it. Climacus thinks that in this process, the system discards the uniqueness of every event and individuality. "World-historically, the individual subject certainly is a trifle, ethically, the individual subject is infinitely important."[66] The world-historical attitude absolutizes the ethical relation through which the subject apotheosizes the social norms of her finite context. The deification of the external situation is, for Climacus, the major threat that may impede the self's achievement of inwardness.

In addition, the world-historical temporalizes the eternal in positing the ethical as the ultimate. According to Climacus, the temporalization of the eternal is the main threat of systematic Philosophy to Christianity because it displaces the infinite. The ethical systematician is driven by the norms from the world process, which she accepts as the manifestation of God. "Therefore God does not play the role of the lord in the world-historical process as it is seen by human beings. Just as one does not see the ethical in it, so also one does not see God, because if he is not seen in the role of the Lord, one does not see him...In the world-historical process, God is metaphysically laced in a half-metaphysical, half-esthetic-dramatic, conventional corset, which is immanence."[67] The immanent account of God represents a double threat. It violates the position of the infinite by relegating it to the temporal. Also, it asserts the ethical individuality as the culmination of immanence; it elevates the ethical individual to divine status as the highest expression of immanence.

The Content and Structure of Subjectivity

Climacus introduces two plausible ways of considering truth. The objective consideration thematizes truth as an object that the objective thinker studies from an abstract perspective. In this process, objectivity is indifferent to the essential relation of truth to a given subjectivity; it removes truth from its subjective counterpart. The subjective consideration of truth—that Climacus favors—is rooted essentially in the subjectivity of the self. Subjective truth cannot be appropriated from the objective stance; it demands existential involvement. Climacus observes that: "To objective reflection, truth becomes something objective, an object, and the point is to disregard the subject. To subjective reflection, truth becomes appropriation, inwardness, subjectivity, and the point is to immerse oneself, existing, in subjectivity."[68] It is noteworthy that the subjective approach to truth—like the issue of subjectivity—calls for the decision to internalize and assume responsibility toward God. The self cannot be objective to subjectivity and truth, which are lived experiences toward which one cannot be indifferent and abstract.

Climacus stresses that the subjective consideration of truth has the virtue of being loyal to the existence of the individual. Subjective truth is sensitive to the existence-relation for which the individual's existence is a never-ending striving. Unlike the world-historical attitude, it does not reach any conclusion about existence. Climacus asserts vehemently that: "All essential knowing pertains to existence, or only the knowing whose relation to existence is essential is essential knowing. Essentially viewed, the knowing that does not inwardly in the reflection of inwardness pertain to existence is accidental knowing, and its degree and scope, essentially viewed, are a matter of indifference."[69] When viewed objectively, the subjective attitude toward truth is absurd. Its absurdity lies in the fact that it is not transparent to the systematic and abstract approach of objectivity. The resistance of subjective truth to objective analysis—which is reminding of the relation of the understanding and the paradox in the *Fragments*—leads to the characterization of truth as the paradox. Climacus explains: "At its highest, inwardness in an existing subject is passion; truth as a paradox corresponds to passion, and that truth becomes a paradox is grounded precisely in its relation to an existing subject."[70] Hence Climacus presents subjective truth from both, the inner perspective of lived experience and the way that objectivity perceives it from without. The fact that subjective truth is grounded in inwardness and remains elusive to the thematization of objectivity makes its structure determinable only by *how* it is lived by the subject. "*Objectively the emphasis is on what is said; subjectively the emphasis is on how it is said*...At its maximum, this 'how' is the passion of the infinite, and the passion of the infinite is the very truth. But the passion of the infinite is precisely subjectivity, and thus subjectivity is truth."[71] Climacus is here subverting the traditional objective view of truth to put forward an account of truth that is inseparable from subjective intensity—the passion of faith.

The Form of the Subjective Thinker

That Climacus's goal in the *CUP* is both, philosophical and religious emerges in the exposition of the ideals of the subjective thinker. Furthermore, the exposition is the theoretical presentation of the embodiment of a thinker in whom the cognitive faculties are put at the service of subjectivity and Christian ethos. Indeed, Climacus's definition that: "for a subjective thinker, imagination, feeling, and dialectics in impassioned existence-inwardness are required."[72] is reminding of the characteristics that he reveres in Lessing's works and biography. Climacus is here presenting theoretically what he presents concretely in the figure of Lessing. As Stott's comment points out:

> In addition to the notion of the individual and the demand for personal decision mentioned previously, Kierkegaard's conception of subjectivity is characterized by the necessity for a passionate personal commitment to truth. In this area Lessing unequivocally embodies the impassioned intensity of the subjectively existing individual. Lessing's entire production and, in actuality, his life itself, is governed by an overriding drive toward the truth.[73]

The subjective thinker is the combination of the aesthetic and religious notions that Climacus asserts. She is the subject who is aware of the limitation of the ethical relation and the demands of the religious relation, as well. The attributes that Climacus ascribes to the subjective thinker suggest that she is the one who is able to manage effectively the three stages of existence—aesthetic, ethical, and religious. One can observe this fact in the statement below, in which Climacus describes existence as an art form:

> Yet the subjective thinker is not a poet even if he is also a poet, not an ethicist even if he is also an ethicist, but is also a dialectician and is himself essentially existing, whereas the poet's existence is inessential in relation to the poem, and likewise the ethicist's in relation to the teaching, and the dialectician's in relation to the thought. The subjective thinker is not a scientific-scholar; he is an artist. To exist is an art. The subjective thinker is esthetic enough for his life to have esthetic content, ethical enough to regulate it, dialectical enough in thinking to master it.[74]

The subjective thinker has the ability to accept the relative within its relative and finite context. However, this fact does not prevent her from being fully immersed in existence, as an aesthetic enterprise. It is noteworthy that Climacus's description of the subjective thinker's responsibility for the stages of existence does not suggest that she is lonely, forlorn, and in despair. The existential attitude of the subjective thinker allows her to be fully immersed in the finitude of life, while maintaining religious inwardness. It is at this juncture that Westphal's comment is helpful in differentiating Climacus's account from existentialism:

> Nor is it [individualism] existentialism's metaphysical rebellion, featuring the individual as a courageous but lonely protest against a Godless, meaningless world. It is ethical-religious subjectivity, featuring the individual as personally responsible for the choice of a certain kind of life and for the choices that stem from that choice. It is especially important to notice that this latter individualism has nothing atomistic about it. On the contrary, it implies that precisely as one whose essence is to exist, in the sense of becoming subjective, I am essentially related both, to God and to neighbor.[75]

Westphal's observation is in order with Climacus's view because the Christian believer is essentially a subjective thinker. The subjective grasp of one's existence and the authentic Christian way of life are the same for Climacus. Climacus is suggesting that subjectivity deepens even the act of thinking, since: "To understand oneself in existence is also *the Christian principle*, except that this *self* has received much richer and much more profound qualifications that are even more difficult to understand together with existing."[76] In the light of this statement, Climacus puts forth the alternative to overcome the antithetical relation of the understanding and the paradox that was previously raised in the *Fragments*. The rational process of understanding is reconciled with being a Christian. Subjective existence makes the achievement of eternal happiness feasible from the historical point of departure. Moreover, the reconciliation occurs in existence—as the unity of the eternal and temporal. The subjective thinker is thus a hybrid of the finite and infinite. Climacus reiterates the issue of the understanding and the paradox, previously raised in the *Fragments*, at this juncture of the text in order to return to the driving question of the *Fragments*: *How can an Eternal Happiness Be Built on Historical Knowledge?* in chapter 4.

The Issue of the Fragments

Climacus returns to the issue of the *Fragments* with the intention to elucidate its infrastructure and the way that the question: *How can an Eternal Happiness Be Built on Historical Knowledge?* was presented. Climacus's justification for using paganism as the starting point to address the issue confirms the fact that the *Fragments* is indeed the attempt to transcend the Hellenic disposition to introduce Christianity. Climacus's choice of paganism, as the basis of the text, is due to the lack of appropriate genuine Christian experience among his contemporaries to start his account of Christianity. Climacus believes that the prevailing of speculative Philosophy's attempt to explain Christianity has abolished every authentic experience of Christianity. Consequently, Christianity can be reintroduced only by starting with the attitude of the understanding to show how Christianity may come about upon its basis.

Climacus is critical of Baptism as the starting point of Christianity because it is merely the traditional possibility that one may achieve the genuine Christian way of life. In addition, Climacus does not consider Baptism as the first stage in Christianity because it has been assimilated in Christendom. "What is Baptism without appropriation? It is the possibility that the baptized child can become a Christian, neither more nor less. The parallel would be: just as one must be born, must have come into existence, in order to become a human being, inasmuch as an infant is not yet that, so one must be baptized in order to become a Christian."[77] Baptism is merely the avenue to become a Christian, which requires subjective appropriation. However, speculative Philosophy undercuts the role of Baptism in allowing one to become a Christian. Speculative Philosophy undermines even the role of Baptism in eliminating the need for inward appropriation to become a Christian via rationalization. "Under such circumstances in Christendom (the dubiousness of speculative thought on the one hand and that one is Christian as a matter of course on the other), it becomes more and more difficult to find a point of departure if one wants to know what Christianity is."[78]

Climacus seems to have recourse to paganism as the starting point of the *Fragments* because it is the natural consequence of speculative Philosophy's explanation of Christianity. Climacus believes that speculative Philosophy's attempt to explain Christianity has been detrimental in bringing it backward. Thus, starting the issue with the discussion of paganism is sensitive to the tendencies of the nineteenth century. Climacus elaborates: "In other words, speculative thought makes paganism the outcome of Christianity, and to be Christian as a matter of course by being baptized changes Christendom into a baptized paganism. That is why I resorted to paganism and to Greece as representative of intellectuality and to its greatest hero, Socrates. After having made sure of paganism, I tried to find in it the most decisive heterogeneity."[79] What Climacus means by 'decisive heterogeneity' is the question regarding the possibility of eternal happiness in History. The achievement of eternal happiness in the never-ending striving of the existence relation is the essentially Christian experience. "That an eternal happiness is decided in time by the relation to something historical was the substance of what was imaginatively constructed and what I now call the essentially Christian."[80]

However, Climacus is emphatic on the fact that the *Fragments* is merely a presentation of the issue of the essentially Christian. The exposition does not solve the issue, but only introduces the inherent difficulty in becoming a Christian. By the same token, Climacus reveals that he is not a Christian, but only aspires to become so. The structure of the text is that in asserting that the decision is to be made in the future, it opens up the possibility that it will be occasioned by inwardness. The structure of the text is meant to grant priority to inwardness over objectivity. "The fact that the decision in the external by which I become a Christian is anticipated has the effect that the decision, if it is made, becomes purely inward and its inwardness therefore even greater than when in addition the decision takes place in the external. The less externality, the more inwardness."[81] Climacus presents Christianity as an inward state of being and not as a doctrine. To emphasize the difference between Christianity as inwardness and Christendom—as a doctrine, Climacus describes it as an arduous path to follow. "The introducing that I take upon myself consists, by repelling, in making it difficult to become a Christian and understands Christianity not as a doctrine but as an existence-contradiction and existence-communication. Therefore, it introduces psychologically, not world-historically, by evoking an awareness of how much must be lived and how difficult it is to become really aware of the difficulty of the decision."[82] The difficulty of becoming a Christian is essentially what differentiates it from prevailing Christendom.

> But if becoming a Christian is the difficulty, the absolute decision, then the only possible introduction is a repelling one that just by the repulsion points out that it is the absolute decision.⁸³

Besides, the difficulty of the text is loyal to the issue itself. Climacus is keen on the fact that the difficulty of the account is not deliberate, but instead agrees with the nature of the topic. According to Climacus, the difficulty is the outcome of the dual constitution of the issue. The issue has both, a passionate and dialectical aspect. The reconciliation of the dialectical and the passionate, as the pathos-filled, constitutes the difficulty of the exposition. "The issue is pathos-filled and dialectical. The pathos is in the first part, since a person's passion culminates in the pathos-filled relation to eternal happiness. The dialectical is in the last part, and the difficulty is precisely that the difficulty is composed in this way."⁸⁴ The elaboration of these two aspects and their combination make up the two final parts of the *CUP*. However, Climacus warns the reader that the decision to become a Christian—as the only way to be set on the path of becoming a Christian—should be made by the individual alone. Climacus may only present how the combination is feasible; it can only be carried out through the self's existential commitment.

> In order to clarify the issue, I shall first of all discuss the pathos-filled and then the dialectical, but I ask the reader continually to recollect that the difficulty finally consists in combining the two, that the existing person who in absolute passion and filled with pathos expresses by his existence his pathos-filled relation to the eternal happiness—must now relate to the dialectical decision.⁸⁵

The Pathos-Filled Relation

Esthetic pathos is different from existential pathos because the former absolutizes the idea and posits the idea as higher than the existence of the self. On the other hand, the pathos-filled subject appropriates the idea in such a way that it transforms subjectivity. The idea is valuable in virtue of its ability to change the self's inward disposition. "Esthetic pathos expresses itself in words and can in its truth signify that the individual abandons himself in order to lose himself in the idea, whereas existential pathos results from the transforming relation of the idea to individual's existence."[86] The idea is thus void independently of the subjective appropriation. According to Climacus, existential pathos derives from the transformation of subjectivity in the attempt to appropriate the highest good, which is the eternal happiness of becoming a Christian. The pathos-filled relation results from the fusion of subjectivity and the idea of becoming a Christian.

The inward transformation of existential pathos requires that the self forsake the comfort of material and finite life. The eternal nature of the goal of being a Christian is in opposition to the relative situation of finitude. In order for the subject to gratify her infinite side, she must limit her involvement in the finite. "Existence is composed of the infinite and the finite; the existing person is infinite and finite. Now, if to him an eternal happiness is his highest good, this means that in his acting the finite elements are once and for all reduced to what must be surrendered in relation to the eternal happiness."[87] The subject's limited involvement in finitude and material comfort is the outward expression of the inward change that the highest good is bringing about. In doing so, the self strives to become commensurate with the relation to the infinite. The consistency of the pathos-filled relation is kept in check by resignation. For Climacus, it is: "When resignation makes a visitation to immediacy, it gives notice that the individual must not have his life in it, and resignation gives it notice of what can happen in life...If, however, the inspecting resignation discovers no irregularity, this shows that the individual at the time of inspection is relating himself to an eternal happiness."[88] Thus the mode of acquisition in the pathos-filled relation is not separable from what is acquired; the acquisition is precisely the striving to reach the essentially Christian itself. Climacus comments on this fact in the following remark:

> Therefore eternal happiness, as the absolute good, has the remarkable quality that it can be defined only by the mode in which it is acquired, whereas other goods, just because the mode of acquisition is accidental or at any rate relatively dialectical must be defined by the good itself...But there is no shortcut to the absolute good, and since it is defined only by the mode of acquisition, the absolute difficulty of this is the only sign that one is relating oneself to the absolute good.[89]

Climacus develops the concrete expressions of the limitation that the pathos-filled relation demands. This aspect is the concretion of the duty to relate infinitely to the infinite and relatively to the relative. The elaboration of the pathos-filled relation in practice is that which differentiates it from strict asceticism. In relating through the pathos-filled relationship the individual is expected to relate relatively to the finite and infinitely to the infinite. "In order to relate himself absolutely to the absolute τέλος, the individual must have practiced renunciation of the relative ends, and only then can there be any question of the ideal task: simultaneously to relate oneself absolutely to the absolute and relatively to the relative."[90] This relationship is different from the yogi's complete forsaking of all earthly means of gratification in search of nirvana. The pathos-filled relationship aspires to establish balance between the finite and the infinite by recognizing the intrinsic worthiness of both.

Climacus is emphasizing the necessity to deal with the relative on relative terms in order to elicit the experience of suffering within inwardness. However, the suffering that Climacus means is different from that of the deprivation of relative ends; suffering is the intensity that subjectivity acquires in the attempt to stretch toward the infinite. As Climacus suggests, it is a negative intensity that points out the positive fact that subjectivity is reaching out to the infinite; suffering represents a mystical experience through which subjectivity strives for wholeness. The essential feature of suffering is spiritual trial.

> Within religious suffering lies the category of spiritual trial, and only there can it be defined...in spiritual trial, it is the higher that, seemingly envious of the individual, wants to frighten him back...Therefore spiritual trial begins only in the sphere of the religious proper, and there only in the final course, and quite rightly increases in proportion to the religiousness because the individual has discovered the boundary, and the spiritual trial expresses the response of the boundary against the finite individual."[91]

Despite of the spiritual trial, Climacus posits that the individual still has to fulfill her ethical responsibility. The fulfillment of ethical duties in the finite domain is feasible through the application of the ironic attitude. The fact that the individual ought to remain ethical is the expression of Climacus's acknowledgment of the necessity to remain appreciative of the social context of the finite; the individual does not become anti-worldly while undergoing the spiritual trial. Irony is the negative standpoint of the consciousness that does not absolutize the finite norms of the state. Climacus insists that although one relates relatively to the ethical, it must nevertheless appear to be absolute. This ability is essential for the genuine ethicist, for Climacus. "The Irony emerges continually joining the particulars of the finite with the ethical infinite requirement and allowing the contradiction to come into existence. The one who can do it with proficiency and not let himself be caught in any relativity, in which its proficiency becomes diffident, must have made the movement of infinity, and to that extent it is possible that he is an ethicist."[92] The ironist has the proper attitude in that he does not allow the ethical to stand between her relationship with the infinite. "Accordingly, Climacus reiterates Kierkegaard's claim in his dissertation that it is the proper task of Irony to deliver us from 'the snares of relativity'."[93] The ironist is the antithesis of the world-historical attitude. It prevents the individual's complete consumption by the world-historical attitude.

The two other dispositions that Climacus introduces in the pathos-filled relation are humor and religiousness. The contradiction between the finite and the infinite that the pathos-filled individual observes is the occasion for the rise of the ironist and humorist attitudes. It is on the basis of this inherent contradiction of the finite situation, that the individual adopts the humorist attitude. "The humorist continually (not in the sense of the pastor's 'always' but at every time of day, wherever he is and whatever he thinks or undertakes) joins the conception of God together with something else and brings out the contradiction—but he does not relate himself to God in religious passion (stricte sic dictus [in te strict sense of the word])."[94] The humorist faces the limitation of not relating to God through subjective passion. The ironist and humorist are not yet religious subjectivities because of their partial belonging to the finite situation. Westphal elucidates these attitudes in the claim that: "The mere ironist and the mere humorist have the same insights as the corresponding ethical and religious tasks implicit in these insights. This means that the mere humorist, while ever so close to the religious, is just as close to cynicism, just as the mere ironist, while ever so close to the ethical, is just as close nihilism."[95] This explanation illustrates that the religious relation is not easily achieved. The ironist and humorist attitudes are illustrations of Climacus's claim to make the issues of the *Fragments* intimidating philosophically via their difficulty.

The religious attitude consists in the transcendence of the finite vestiges that impede the humorist and ironist. It is the consciousness of being always before the infinite gaze. Thus, the religious disposition performs all earthly duties with the constant awareness of the infinite as its point of reference. In agreement with the religious disposition, the self's complete involvement in the finite setting is the outcome of compliance to a divine injunction.[96] Climacus describes the religious attitude in the following: "Therefore, the religiousness with humor as the incognito is the unity of absolute religious passion (inwardly deepened dialectically) and spiritual maturity, which calls religiousness back from all outwardness into inwardness and therein it is again indeed the absolute religious passion."[97] The privileged status of the religious attitude lies in the possession of the guilt-consciousness. The guilt-consciousness that Climacus asserts as the fundamental feature of the pathos-filled relation is the manifestation of one's complete involvement in existence. "Thus the essential consciousness of guilt is the greatest possible immersion in existence, and it also expresses that an existing person relates himself to an eternal happiness (The childish and comparative guilt-consciousness relates itself to itself and to the comparative), expresses the relation by expressing the misrelation."[98] The shortcoming of the humorist and ironist lies precisely in the failure to manifest the misrelation. In the religious attitude, the individual is aware that her relation is a misrelation because she appears to be relating to the finite while she is genuinely relating to the infinite. Guilt-consciousness is the awareness that one is always relating to infinity before which one is inferior. Thus, every finite undertaking is carried out before the watchful eye of the infinite *Other*.

Climacus then presents two ways through which the religious attitude may be substantiated. Being essentially a disposition, the religious attitude that springs from the pathos-filled relation may remain strictly as inward deepening. In this event, inwardness revolves upon itself and acquires intensity by deepening the infinite relation from within. Climacus characterizes this form of the religious as *Religiousness A*. "Religiousness A is the dialectic of inward deepening; it is the relation to an eternal happiness that is not conditioned by a something but is the dialectical inward deepening of the relation, consequently conditioned only by the inward deepening, which is dialectical."[99] Thus, Climacus—through the assertion of Religiousness A—allows the possibility that religiosity may remain free of all external conditioning; it is essentially bound within subjectivity. Moreover, Religiousness A represents the disposition on the basis of which one chooses to become part of a specific religious dogma. On the other hand, Religiousness B is the disposition of Religiousness A that is being conditioned by the essentially Christian as a transcendent. Religiousness B, as the apex of the individual's religious subjectivity, is preceded by Religiousness A. Climacus describes it in the following:

> On the other hand Religiousness B, as it will be called from now on, or paradoxical religiousness, as it has been called, or the religiousness that has the dialectical in second place, makes conditions in such a way that the conditions are not the dialectical concentrations of inward deepening but a definite something that qualifies the eternal happiness more specifically (whereas in A the more specific qualification of inward deepening is the only more specific qualification), not by qualifying more specifically the individual's appropriation of it but by qualifying more specifically the eternal happiness, yet not as a task for thinking but as paradoxically repelling and giving rise to new pathos.[100]

The Qualitative Dialectic

Climacus describes the appropriate use of the rational faculties in relation to the essentially Christian by elaborating the notion of the qualitative dialectic. This deed is in accord with the overall aim of the *Fragments* in that it wishes to grant the understanding its appropriate function in relation to the paradox. According to Climacus, the understanding remains a legitimate constituent within individuality in acknowledging that the paradox—the essentially Christian—remains incomprehensible to the cognitive faculties. Climacus, firstly, provides the contrast of the qualitative dialectic as the *revivalist*. The revivalist is animated by a contradiction. The contradiction consists in the fact that the revivalist wishes to convey the experience of inwardness through the means of the understanding. It is a comic attitude that wants to explain the passionate by the means of the cognitive. "The contradiction in the arrogating revivalist is that he, after having through faith entered into the innermost sanctum of inwardness against his understanding, also wants to be out on the street and be matchlessly brilliant."[101] The revivalist attitude is another form of the misuse of faith—described in the *Fragments*—that tries to appropriate the god via contemporaries' account and historical data.

On the other hand, the qualitative dialectic attitude acknowledges that the understanding comes to a halt before the paradox. The paradox cannot be grasped nor accounted for by the means of the understanding. The qualitative dialectic preserves the understanding as the antithesis of belief. In virtue of the qualitative dialectic the individual is aware that genuine belief requires its opposite; for belief to be possible, the understanding must exist as well. Climacus explains the dynamics of the qualitative dialectic in the following:

> Consequently the believing Christian both, has and uses his understanding, respects the universally human, does not explain someone's not becoming a Christian as a lack of understanding, but believes Christianity against the understanding and here uses the understanding—in order to see to it that he believes against the understanding. Therefore, he cannot believe nonsense against the understanding, which one might fear, because the understanding will penetratingly perceive that it is nonsense and hinder him in believing it, but he uses the understanding so much that through it he becomes aware of the incomprehensible, and now, believing, he relates himself to it against the understanding.[102]

The paradox that remains elusive to the understanding is the contradiction that the eternal becomes manifest in time. It stresses the role of subjective existence that becomes the bearer of the eternal in time. "To exist as a Christian from day to day is as great a struggle as becoming a Christian. There is always the risk that one will lose faith and fall away. It is important to keep the two elements of becoming and existing as a Christian in mind if we are to understand what Kierkegaard is about in his work."[103] The paradox is loyal to the challenge of remaining a Christian. By occasioning the expectation of eternal happiness in the temporal relation, the paradox is essentially in opposition to the understanding. "*The paradoxical-religious* defines the distinction absolutely by paradoxically accentuating existing. In other words, because the eternal has come into existence at a moment of time, the existing individual in time does not relate himself to the eternal or to collect himself in his relation (this is A) but *in time* comes to relate himself to the eternal *in time*."[104] The paradoxical-religious is the dialectic through which Religiousness A transcends its subjective boundaries. For Climacus, eternal happiness becomes the transcendent for Religiousness A because it is now situated in a specific point in time through the paradoxical-religious.

However, Climacus is cautious regarding the possibility that in the paradoxical-religious relation, the situation of the eternal in time may be posited as definite. The manifestation of the eternal in the historical is never fixed; the historical to which the subject relates is always an approximation. For Climacus, the eternal is never isomorphic with the historical. History is only approximation. "The contradiction is to base one's eternal happiness on an approximation, which can be done only if one has no eternal qualification in oneself (which in turn cannot be thought any more than how one then comes to think of it; therefore the god must provide the condition), which is why this in turn is coherent with the paradoxical accentuation of existence."[105] Furthermore, this contradiction is consistent with the individual's existence as well. Existence is never entirely commensurate with its objective social setting; existence always has some excess over the objective social domain in which it manifests itself.

However, the historical—as approximation—is not a universal to which every individual relates equally. The historical—as the occasion for the god to give the condition—is to be appropriated by every individual according to the *how* of her subjective life. The god gives the condition anew to every member of each generation. It is on the basis of this unique relation of the god to each individual that the notions of the followers at first hand and followers at second hand were annulled in the *Fragments*. Climacus believes that if the historical as the coming of the eternal in time is posited as a universal that is valid for all, then the religious aspect is superseded by an anthropological event. Christianity is thus transformed into anthropology. Climacus concludes his explanation by suggesting that this fact occurs in speculative Philosophy that culminates in the metaphysics of speculative Philosophy.

> If, however, the coming into existence of the eternal in time is supposed to be an eternal coming into existence, then Religiousness B is abolished, 'all theology is anthropology,' Christianity is changed from an existence-communication into an ingenious metaphysical doctrine addressed to professors, and Religiousness A is prinked up with an esthetic-metaphysical ornamentation that in categorical respects neither adds nor detracts.[106]

Humor and the Issue of Christianity

Hitherto, Climacus has delineated the ideal subjective thinker through Gothold Lessing and his antithesis as Hegel—the prototype of objective thinking. The question that is yet to be answered is regarding the nature of the author of the exposition himself: Is Climacus a subjective thinker or is he a Christian? In the two sections—*An Understanding with the Reader and A First and Last Explanation*—at the end of the *CUP*, Climacus wishes to clarify his status. Climacus reveals that he is a humorist. This declaration is important to understand the nature of Climacus as a pseudonym and its relation to the exposition. By the same token, it elucidates the Preface of the *Fragments* that emphasizes the pseudonymous nature of Climacus. To recapitulate, the humorist has come to develop the inward disposition through Religiousness A. She has acquired the proper conception of God through religious passion. The shortcoming of the humorist is that she has not fully overcome her finite heritage, to which she continually relates her religious passion. Climacus states:

> The undersigned, Johannes Climacus, who has written this book, does not make out that he is a Christian; for he is, to be sure, completely preoccupied with how difficult it must be to become one; but even less is he one who, after having been a Christian, ceases to be that by going further. He is a humorist; satisfied with his circumstances at the moment, hoping that something better will befall his lot, he feels especially happy, if worst comes to worst, to be born in this speculative, theocentric century.[107]

Climacus has certainly the inward deepening relation to the infinite of Religiousness A. The fact that he is concerned with the 'difficulty of becoming a Christian' and his satisfaction with his 'present circumstances at the moment' represent the finite aspect—as the transcendent—which prevents Climacus from being a Christian. That Climacus is indeed religiously disposed is revealed in Kierkegaard's *The Point of View for my Work as an Author* published three years later after the *CUP* in 1849. Kierkegaard makes the following claim regarding the author of the *Postscript*: "I could express myself very briefly even with regard to the *Concluding Postscript*, since that book does not present any difficulties when the point of view for the literary work as a whole is that the author is a religious author."[108] Hence, Climacus is aware that the inward relation of Religiousness A cannot overcome the difficulties of becoming a Christian. The implication of Religiousness A is that "eternal life for Kierkegaard is intelligible only through a *metabasis in all geno* a fundamental change in the *way* that we think about ourselves."[109] The subjective transformation must relate to Religiousness B in order for eternal happiness to be achievable. The awareness of the essentially Christian as the transcendent that is necessary to become a Christian is insufficient as well, since the subject has to live Religiousness B and not merely conceptualize it.

Under the light of the two concluding sections, it becomes evident that Climacus has a twofold relation with the *Fragments* and *Postscript*. Johannes Climacus is simultaneously the author and the incarnation of the issue of the texts. Climacus is the author of the works as the mouthpiece that presents the issue: Whether eternal happiness is achievable on the basis of historical knowledge and the personification of the difficulty of this possibility as well. Climacus boldly claims that: "In the isolation of the imaginary construction, the whole book is about myself, simply and solely about myself."[110] The aesthetic accomplishment and the uniqueness of the Kierkegaardian corpus consist in the fact that the individuality of each pseudonym is drawn out in the exposition itself; the pseudonymous author stands as the embodiment of the issue of the exposition.

> What has been written, then, is mine, but only insofar as I, by means of audible lines, have placed the life-view of the creating, poetically actual individuality in his mouth, for my relation is even more remote than that of a poet, who *poetizes* characters and yet in the preface is *himself* the *author*. That is, I am impersonally or personally in the third person a *souffleur* [prompter] who has poetically produced the *authors*, whose *prefaces* in turn are their productions, as their *names* are also.[111]

Conclusion

The philosophic-theological exposition of both, the *Philosophical Fragments* and *Concluding Unscientific Postscript* revolves around the question: How Can Eternal Happiness Be Built on Historical Knowledge? This question is pivotal for the restoration of the autonomy of Kierkegaard's philosophical project. The development of the arguments in the *Fragments* and *CUP* shows that Climacus is engaged in developing the dominant notions of Kierkegaard's Philosophy around the attempt to provide an answer to this question. Throughout the treatment of the question, Climacus relies on Irony as a Romantic notion. Moreover, his ongoing conversation with Kantian and Hegelian concepts is consistent with his view of Kant and Hegel as the pioneers and culmination of German Idealism and Modern Philosophy. By presenting his own notions, while being critical of the Idealist concepts of Kant and Hegel, Climacus discloses his philosophical heritage from this tradition in being critical of it. Also, the issue of the *Fragments* and *Postscript* is recurrent in other pseudonymous works of Kierkegaard. The relation of subjectivity and genuine Christianity is at the center of Kierkegaard's entire corpus. Thus, the attempt to assimilate any Kierkegaardian notion independently of the above question and the relation of subjectivity and Christianity may only lead to a partial reading of Kierkegaard's philosophical goal.

On the other hand, the development of the arguments of the *Fragments* and *CUP* demonstrates that Climacus's polemical attitude toward the Hegelian system is consistent throughout. The system or speculative Philosophy plays the role of a backdrop upon which Climacus presents the way that subjectivity, in relating to Christianity, achieves eternal happiness on the basis of History. Hegelian speculative Philosophy is the foil against which the infrastructure of subjectivity's relation to Christianity is developed. For Climacus, the inclination of the age that results from the prevalence of speculative Philosophy to assimilate Christianity is that which leads to the rise of Christendom—or spiritlessness. Viewed from Climacus's perspective, Hegelian Philosophy is essentially the propagation of spiritlessness. Therefore, to think that Kierkegaard's philosophical project would not have been possible independently of its commonality with that of Hegel is a misreading of Kierkegaard's polemical attitude toward Hegelian Philosophy. Mark Taylor's *Journeys to Selfhood* errs in arguing in favor of the commonality between Hegel's and Kierkegaard's philosophical projects. Taylor's reading makes Kierkegaard's Philosophy too Hegelian and Hegel's Philosophy too Kierkegaardian; it misreads both.

Furthermore, Climacus's presentation of Religiousness A opens up the possibility to reflect upon the religious attitude of the Modern self. Religiousness A is essentially limited to the subjective domain; relating inwardly to eternal happiness intensifies it. Climacus's account of Religiousness A can elucidate the attempt to understand the Modern attitude toward religion. Let us consider a statement of Climacus regarding Religiousness A: "Religiousness A can be present in paganism, and in Christianity it can be the religiousness of everyone who is not decisively Christian, whether baptized or not."[112] In this statement, Climacus makes it clear that Religiousness A may prevail in non-Christian context as well. Religiousness A represents the subjective preparation to become religious; it is the *being able* to become Christian.

Climacus's account of Religiousness A is here relevant to the Modern perspective on religion in the Modern context in asserting that subjectivity is not intrinsically linked with the dominant religious belief of its social context. Climacus allows religious belief to be based on individual subjective acceptance rather than authority. One must develop the subjective disposition prior to committing to any set of religious beliefs. In Modernity, the subject does not accept religion blindly; the Modern self has the privilege of contemplating the religious beliefs before relating to them as subjective guidelines. If we agree with Henriksen's definition that: "Modernity means a critical reaction against any traditionally given content. Hence it demands a mode of reflection that makes religion and religious beliefs transparent and viable in their present forms."[113] we can observe that Climacus's account of Religiousness A is precisely the disposition that makes this critical reflection feasible.

In addition, the individual's critical attitude toward religion and religious beliefs rules out the tyranny of religious authority. The individual becomes the decisive authority in religious matters because she alone decides to comply or refute the religious beliefs that are available. "An element in the Modern appropriation – or rejection – of religion is that it can no longer be taken for granted. This is the natural consequence of what has been said so far. Some describe this as *the problem of authority*. In Modernity, there is no other authority than the subject and what the subject can make her own."[114]

The individual's authority is based upon her ability to appropriate religion according to subjective passion. It is in virtue of this accomplishment that Climacus's account in these two texts is a pioneer in deconstructing the tyranny of religious dogma and in restoring autonomy to the believer as a free subjectivity. In addition, Climacus's account is helpful for the status of Christianity in Modernity as well. Religiousness A—as inward deepening and the religion of immanence—creates the opportunity to accept Christianity in freedom. Religiousness B, as the religion of transcendence—is a commitment to Christianity that takes place in total freedom. In the exposition of the issue of the *Fragments* and *Postscript*, Climacus, thus, provides the path to a deeper and free commitment to Christianity in Modernity that depends upon the individual's subjective commitment.

Notes

Kierkegaard's Critique of Romanticism and German Idealism

1. Soren Kierkegaard, *The Concept of Irony: with continual reference to Socrates,* trans. Howard Hong &Edna Hong (Princeton University Press, 1989), p. 272-3. Heretofore will be cited as *CI*.
2. *CI,* 273
3. *CI,* 273
4. *CI,* 273
5. *CI,* 273
6. *CI,* 274
7. *CI,* 275
8. *CI,* 275 see footnote
9. *CI,* 275
10. *CI,* 275-6
11. Manfred Frank, *The Philosophical Foundations of Early German Romanticism,* trans. Elizabeth Millan-Zaibert (State University of New York Press, 2004), p. 34.
12. *CI,* 283
13. Ronald Green, *Kierkegaard and Kant: The Hidden Debt* (SUNY Press, 1992), p. 77.
14. Soren Kierkegaard, *Philosophical Fragments,* trans. Howard Hong & Edna Hong (Princeton University Press, 1985), p. 231.
15. Antoinette Stafford, *Kant and Kierkegaard: The Subjectivization of Faith,* (www.mun.ca/animus/1998vol3/staford3.htm), par. 35
16. Immanuel Kant, *Religion Within the Limits of Reason Alone,* trans. Theodore M. Greene & Hoyt H. Hudson (Harper Torchbooks, 1960), p. 7.
17. C. Stephen Evans, "Kant and Kierkegaard on the Possibility of Metaphysics," in *Kant and Kierkegaard on Religion,* ed. Dewi Z. Phillips and Timothy Tessin (Palgrave Macmillan, 2000), p. 47.
18. Alastair Hannay, *Kierkegaard* (Routledge, 1982), p. 93.
19. Alastair Hannay, *Kierkegaard: A Biography* (Cambridge University Press, 2001), p. 195.
20. Ulrich Knappe, *Theory and Practice in Kant and Kierkegaard* (Walter de Gruyter, 2004), p. 18.
21. Soren Kierkegaard, *Concluding Unscientific Postscript,* trans. Howard Hong & Edna Hong (Princeton University Press, 1992), p. 328.
22. Soren Kierkegaard, *Philosophical Fragments,* trans. Howard Hong & Edna Hong (Princeton University Press, 1985), p. 231.
23. Soren Kierkegaard, *Concluding Unscientific Postscript,* trans. Howard Hong & Edna Hong (Princeton University Press, 1992), p. 335.

Climacus's *Philosophical Fragments*

1. Soren Kierkegaard, *Philosophical Fragments,* trans. Howard Hong &Edna Hong (Princeton University Press, 1985), p. 5. Heretofore will be cited as *PF.*
2. *PF,* 6
3. *PF,* 7
4. *PF,* 7
5. Hugh S. Pyper, "The Lesson of Eternity: Christ as a Teacher in Kierkegaard and Hegel" in *Philosophical Fragments and Johannes Climacus,* Robert Perkins (Mercer University Press, 1994), p. 130.
6. *PF,* 8
7. *PF,* 8
8. *PF,* 9
9. *PF,* 186
10. *PF,* 9 Vigilius Haufniensis elaborates upon the difference between Hellenic and Christian ignorance in the *Concept of Anxiety.* For Haufniensis, Hellenic ignorance can be remedied by recollection because the notion of original sin was foreign to the Greeks. The individual is thus intrinsically worthy of knowledge since there was no Fall and grace was not necessary for the individual to know the truth. On the other hand, Christian ignorance is rooted in the Fall, occasioned by original sin, which makes divine grace an absolute necessity for the individual to know the truth.
11. *PF,* 9-10
12. *PF,* 10
13. *PF,* 10
14. *PF,* 10
15. *PF,* 11
16. *PF,* 11
17. *PF,* 11
18. *PF,* 12
19. *PF,* 12
20. *PF,* 13
21. *PF,* 13
22. *PF,* 13
23. *PF,* 13 my emphasis
24. *PF,* 14
25. *PF,* 14
26. *PF,* 14
27. *PF,* 14
28. *PF,* 14-5
29. *PF,* 15
30. Jacob Howland, *Kierkegaard and Socrates: A Study in Philosophy and Faith* (Cambridge University Press, 2006), p. 29.
31. *PF,* 15
32. *PF,* 15
33. *PF,* 17
34. Soren Kierkegaard, *The Concept of Anxiety,* trans. By Reidar Thomte & Albert Anderson (Princeton University Press, 1980), p. 41. Heretofore will be cited as *CA.*
35. *PF,*16

36. *PF*, 17
37. *PF*, 18
38. *PF*, 18
39. *PF*, 18
40. *PF*, see historical introduction, 18
41. Alastair Hannay, *Kierkegaard: A Biography* (Cambridge University Press, 2001), p. 13. Heretofore will be cited as *Hannay*.
42. Manfred Frank, *The Philosophical Foundations of Early German Romanticism*, trans. Elizabeth Milan-Zaibert (State University of New York Press, 2004), p. 28. Heretofore will be cited as *Frank*.
43. *PF*, 23
44. *PF*, 24
45. *PF*, 24
46. George Stack, *On Kierkegaaard: Philosophical Fragments* (New Jersey: Humanities Press, 1976), p. 15.
47. *PF*, 24-5
48. *PF*, 25
49. *PF*, 25
50. *PF*, 29
51. *PF*, 30
52. *PF*, 30
53. *PF*, 31
54. *PF*, 31
55. *PF*, 32-3
56. *PF*, 33-4
57. *PF*, 34
58. *PF*, 35
59. *PF*, 36
60. *PF*, 23
61. *PF*, 24
62. *PF*, 282. See note 4
63. G.W.F. Hegel, *Lectures on the History of Philosophy*, trans. E.S. Haldane & Frances H. Simson (Routledge & Kegan Paul LTD, 1955), p. 420. Heretofore will be cited as *LHP*.
64. *LHP*, 421-2
65. *LHP*, 422
66. *CI*, 225.
67. *LHP*, 414
68. *CI*, 226
69. *CI*, 227
70. *CI*, 228
71. *CI*, 228
72. Sarah Kofman, *Socrates: Fictions of a Philosopher*, trans. Catherine Porter (Cornell University Press, 1998), p.134.
73. *PF*, 37
74. *PF*, 37
75. *PF*, 38
76. *PF*, 39
77. *PF*, 39

78. *PF*, 39
79. *PF*, 39
80. *PF*, 39-40
81. *PF*, 40
82. *PF*, 41
83. *PF*, 41
84. *PF*, 41 please see footnote
85. *PF*, 41 please see footnote
86. *PF*, 42
87. *PF*, 42
88. *PF*, 42
89. George Pattison, *The Philosophy of Kierkegaard* (McGill Queen's University Press, 2005), p. 14.
90. *PF*, 42-3
91. *PF*, 43
92. *PF*, 43
93. *PF*, 44
94. *PF*, 44
95. *PF*, 44
96. *PF*, 44-5
97. *PF*, 45
98. *PF*, 45
99. *PF*, 45
100. *PF*, 46
101. *PF*, 46
102. *PF*, 46
103. *PF*, 47
104. *PF*, 47
105. *PF*, 190 see *draft* 40:12-30
106. Immanuel Kant, *Critique of Pure Reason*, tr. Norman Kemp Smith (London & New York: Macmillan, 1929), p. 503-04.
107. Ibid., p. 504
108. *PF*, 40
109. *PF*, 41
110. *PF*, 41
111. G.W.F. Hegel, *The Science of Logic*,tr. A. V. Miller. (New York Humanities Press, 1969), p. 89. Heretofore will be cited as *Logic*.
112. *Logic*, 89
113. *Logic*, 90
114. *PF*, 49
115. *PF*, 49
116. *PF*, 49 see footnote
117. *PF*, 50
118. *PF*, 50
119. *PF*, 51
120. *PF*, 51
121. *PF*, 51
122. *PF*, 51
123. *PF*, 51

124. *PF*, 52
125. *PF*, 58
126. *PF*, 55
127. *PF*, 55-6
128. *PF*, 58
129. *PF*, 64
130. *PF*, 64 see footnote
131. *PF*, 59
132. *PF*, 59
133. *PF*, 61
134. Climacus's discussion is reminding of Derrida's account of the repression of the Platonic and the orgiastic in Christianity within Western History in the *Gift of Death*, tr. David Wills (University of Chicago Press, 1995) Climacus is here delineating the dynamics of the transition from the Platonic to the orgiastic of the Christian.
135. *PF*, 62
136. *PF*, 62
137. *PF*, 62
138. Bruce. Kirmmse, *Encounters with Kierkegaard: A Life as Seen by His Contemporaries*, Collected, Edited, and Annotated by Bruce Kirmmse; translated by Bruce Kirmmse &Virginia Laursen (Princeton University Press, 1996), p. 251. Heretofore will be cited as *EWK*.
139. Immanuel Kant, *Critique of Pure Reason*, Ed. & trans, Paul Guyer & Allen Wood (Cambridge Univesity Press, 1998), p. 111. Heretofore will be cited as *CPR*
140. *CPR*, 112
141. *CPR*, 114
142. *CPR*, 116
143. *CPR*, 117
144. *PF*, 60
145. *PF*, 61
146. Paul Ricoeur, *Philosophy after Kierkegaard*, in *Kierkegaard a Critical Reader*, ed. Jonathan Ree & Jane Chamberlain (Massachussets: Blackwell Publishers Inc., 1998), p. 16. Heretofore will be cited as Ricoeur
147. Soren Kierkegaard, *The Sickness Unto Death*, trans. Howard Hong & Edna Hong (Princeton University Press, 1980), p. 82. Heretofore will be cited as *SUD*.
148. *SUD*, 77
149. Anti-Climacus is using 'willing' instead of explicitly citing the understanding because the *SUD* is a Christian-psychological exposition. Anti-Climacus is dealing with the rational faculty, which is the understanding in Climacus's philosophical project, from a strictly psychological-existential perspective. Also, within the Christian context of the *SUD*, Anti-Climacus cites God explicitly whereas, God is a concept in the *Fragments* and the god is the paradox to the understanding.
150. *Hannay*, 239
151. *PF*, 73
152. *PF*, 73
153. *PF*, 73
154. *PF*, 74
155. *PF*, 74
156. *PF*, 74
157. *PF*, 74

158. *PF,* 74
159. *PF,* 74
160. *PF,* 74
161. *PF,* 74-5
162. *PF,* 75
163. *PF,* 75
164. *Stack,* 15
165. *PF,* 75
166. *PF,* 75
167. *PF,* 75
168. *PF,* 75-6
169. *PF,* 76
170. *PF,* 76
171. *PF,* 76
172. *PF,* 76
173. *PF,* 77
174. *PF,* 77
175. *PF,* 77
176. *PF,* 77
177. *PF,* 77-8
178. *PF,* 79
179. *PF,* 79
180. *PF,* 80
181. *PF,* 81
182. *PF,* 81
183. *PF,* 83
184. *PF,* 84
185. *PF,* 86
186. *PF,* 13
187. *Logic,* 543
188. *Logic,* 544
189. *Logic,* 545
190. *Logic,* 545
191. *Logic,* 546
192. *Logic,* 549
193. *PF,* 74
194. *PF,* 89
195. *PF,* 90
196. *PF,* 91
197. *PF,* 91
198. *PF,* 92
199. *PF,* 93
200. *PF,* 93-4
201. *PF,* 94
202. *PF,* 95
203. *PF,* 98
204. *PF,* 98
205. *PF,* 99
206. *PF,* 99

207. *PF,* 99-100
208. *PF,* 100
209. *PF,* 101
210. *PF,* 101
211. *PF,* 102
212. *PF,* 102
213. *PF,* 103
214. *PF,* 109
215. Stephen Mulhall, *Faith and Reason* (Gerald Duckworth & Co., 1994), p. 34.
216. *PF,* 111
217. Gotthold E. Lessing, *Lessing's Theological Writings,* trans. Henry Chadwick (Stanford University Press, 1957), p. 51. Heretofore will be cited as *Lessing.*
218. *Lessing,* 52
219. *Lessing,* 52
220. *Lessing,* 52
221. *Lessing,* 53
222. *Lessing,* 53
223. *Lessing,* 54
224. *Lessing,* 54
225. *Lessing,* 55
226. *Lessing,* 55
227. *PF,* 109

Climacus's *Concluding Unscientific Postscript*

1. Soren Kierkegaard, *Concluding Unscientific Postscript,* trans. Howard Hong & Edna Hong (Princeton University Press, 1992), p. 10. Heretofore will be cited as *CUP.*
2. *CUP,* 10
3. *CUP,* 15
4. *CUP,* 15
5. *CUP,* 17
6. *CUP,* 21
7. Merold Westphal, *Becoming A Self: A Reading of Kierkegaard's Concluding Unscientific Postscript* (Purdue University Press, 1996), p. 49. Heretofore will be cited as *BaS.*
8. *CUP,* 23
9. *CUP,* 24-5
10. *CUP,* 25 see footnote
11. *CUP,* 32-3
12. *CUP,* 34-5
13. *CUP,* 36
14. *CUP,* 38
15. *CUP,* 48
16. *CUP,* 50
17. *CUP,* 52
18. *CUP,* 53
19. *PF,* 81
20. *CUP,* 55
21. *CUP,* 64

22. Michelle Stott, *Behind the Mask:Kierkegaard's Pseudonymic Treatment of Lessing in the Concluding Unscientific Postscript* (Associated University Presses, 1993), p. 95. Heretofore will be cited as *Stott*.
23. *BaS*, 60
24. *CUP*, 65
25. *CUP*, 68
26. David Gouwens, *Kierkegaard as Religious Thinker* (Cambridge University Press, 1996), p. 45. Heretofore will be cited as *Gouwens*.
27. *CUP*, 65-6
28. *BaS*, 60
29. *CUP*, 70 see footnote
30. *BaS*, 49
31. *CUP*, 72
32. *Stott*, 93
33. *CUP*, 72
34. *CUP*, 72-3
35. *CUP*, 73
36. *CUP*, 77
37. *CUP*, 79
38. *CUP*, 74
39. Jan Rogan, *'Keeping Silent Through Speaking'* in *Kierkegaard on Art and Communication*, ed. George Pattison (St. Martin's Press, 1992), p. 97.
40. *CUP*, 79
41. *CUP*, 79-80
42. *CUP*, 80
43. *CUP*, 80
44. *CUP*, 81
45. *CUP*, 92
46. *CUP*, 92
47. *CUP*, 93
48. *CUP*, 95
49. *CUP*, 99
50. *CUP*, 103
51. *CUP*, 105
52. *CUP*, 106
53. *CUP*, 108
54. *BaS*, 91
55. *CUP*, 110
56. *CUP*, 112
57. *CUP*, 118
58. Shmuel H. Bergman, *Dialogical Philosophy from Kierkegaard to Buber* (SUNY Press, 1991), p.15.
59. *CUP*, 119
60. *CUP*, 129
61. *CUP*, 130
62. *CUP*, 133
63. *CUP*, 133
64. *CUP*, 135-6
65. *CUP*, 137

66. *CUP,* 148
67. *CUP,* 156
68. *CUP,* 192
69. *CUP,* 197
70. *CUP,* 199
71. *CUP,* 202-3
72. *CUP,* 350
73. *Stott,* 41
74. *CUP,* 351
75. *BaS,* 140
76. *CUP,* 353
77. *CUP,* 366
78. *CUP,* 368
79. *CUP,* 368
80. *CUP,* 369
81. *CUP,* 382
82. *CUP,* 383
83. *CUP,* 384
84. *CUP,* 385
85. *CUP,* 386
86. *CUP,* 387
87. *CUP,* 391
88. *CUP,* 395
89. *CUP,* 426-7
90. *CUP,* 431-2
91. *CUP,* 458-9
92. *CUP,* 502
93. *BaS,* 166
94. *CUP,* 505
95. *BaS,* 168
96. The religious attitude is further illustrated in *Works of Love* in which the duty to love one's neighbor, even after death, is to be carried out in conformity with the divine injunction to love one's neighbor. The exposition of *Works of Love,* suggests Kierkegaard's belonging to the tradition of the metaphysicians of infinite presence. The neighbor is the presence of infinity in the immediate other, although the presence excesses the finite form of the other. Like Buber's *I and Thou,* Levinas *Totality and Infinity,* Kierkegaard's *Works of Love* is an elaboration of the presence of the infinite Other in the immediate other.
97. *CUP,* 506
98. *CUP,* 531
99. *CUP,* 556
100. *CUP,* 556
101. *CUP,* 565
102. *CUP,* 568
103. David E. Mercer, *Kierkegaard's Living-room: The Relation Between Faith and History in the Philosophical Fragments* (McGill-Queen's Press, 2001), p. 31.
104. *CUP,* 570
105. *CUP,* 574
106. *CUP,* 579
107. *CUP,* 617

108. Soren Kierkegaard, *The Point of View for my Work as an Author*, trans. Walter Lowrie (Harper Torchbook, 1962), p. 42.
109. John H. Whittaker, "Kant and Kierkegaard on Eternal Life" in *Kant and Kierkegaard on Religion*, ed. Dewi Z. Phillips and Timothy Tessin (Palgrave Macmillan, 2000), p. 188.
110. *CUP*, 617
111. *CUP*, 625-6
112. *CUP*, 557
113. Jan-Olav Henriksen, *The Reconstruction of Religion: Lessing, Kierkegaard, and Nietzsche* (Eerdmans Publishing Company, 2001), p. 5.
114. Ibid., p. 8

Index

Adam, 3, 9
Aristotle, 2, 31–32, 66–67
Baptism, 114
Christianity,14–15,27–30,32,48,55–56,59,82–87,91–97,100–102,106–110, 112–117,120–124,126–128
Condition,3,14,26–29,31,38–39,48–49,56–57,59,75,79,82–83,88,91–92,101,120,122
Consciouness,1–2,12,25,36–38,47–48,55–56,63,83–84,91,105,118–120
Contemporary followers,56,59–60,73,76–78,80,82,85,88,89,97,122
Critique, 2, 5, 15, 19, 49, 60–61, 66–67, 73, 101,129
Descartes, 13
Docetism, 7
Epistemological, 2–3, 6 , 12, 14, 21, 25–26, 47, 54, 60
Eternal, 1–5,15,17–18,22–24,29,32–33,49,55–60,62,69,71,76,79,81, 83–84,88, 91–97,105–106,108,110,113–117,119–124,126–127
Eve, 3
Faith, 3–4,8,11,19,46,56–63,73,76–88,91,93–95,97,106,108–109,111,121–122
Followers at second hand, 59, 73, 76–78, 80, 82, 85, 88–89, 97,122
German Idealism, 5–7, 10,11,14,17,30,60,63,126
Hammann, 60
Happiness,1–2,4–5,11,15,17–18,23–24,49,55–59,62,83,88,91–97, 105–106,108,113–117,119–120,122,124,126–127
Hegel, 6, 8, 10–15, 35–38, 49–52, 60, 67, 73–76, 98,100–101,107–108,123,126–127
Hellenic, 4, 22, 28–31, 36, 48, 55–56, 58–59, 82–83, 86
Historical, 1–5,8–9,11,15,18–24,29,31–32,34–35,56–60,62–63,68–73,76–88,90–102,105–106,108–111,113,115,118,121–122,124,126
History,2,13,17,23,32–33,35–36,49,55–56,64,68–69,71,84–86,92–96,114,122,126

Humorist, 9–10, 19, 119–120,123
Ignorance, 3
Immanentism, 11–12
Immanent, 1–2, 11–12, 18, 110
Irony, 2, 5–10, 14, 18, 30, 36, 38, 90, 99–100,118,126
Jacobi, 60
Jesus Christ, 3–4, 33, 84
Kant, 5–8, 10–13, 46, 49, 50–52, 60–63, 98,126
Kierkegaard, 4–15,17–18,23,30,32,36–38,42–43,60,63–64,83,87,94,98–99, 106–107,109,112,118,122,124,126–127,129
Knowledge, 1–3,5,8–10,12-13,18,21,232–24,36,38–40,43,45,55,60–63,65,67, 72–73, 81, 91, 94, 98, 102–105,113,121,124,126
Leap, 3, 43, 44, 80, 87–88, 95, 106, 108
Learner, 2–4, 23–35, 39–40, 55–59, 62, 82–83
Lessing, 60, 84–89, 98–102,104–109,112,123
Messiah, 4
Modern Philosophy, 2, 4–5, 10, 12–15, 17, 126
Moment, 2,4,8,19,24–26,28–30,32–33,35,38,40–41,43,48,54–59,65,84,86,95,110,122–124
Paradox, 1,15,39,40,43,44,47,48,52–60, 62–64, 69,73–74, 80,87,95,106,111,113,120–122
Philosophy, 6–7,10–14,17,19,23,36,39,46,63,92–93,95–97,101,110,114,123, 126–127
Platonic, 2, 21, 22
Possibility, 2,8,15,32,43–44,46–49,51,57,60,65–67,69–70,72–76,78,81,86,106–108,114–115,120,122,124,127
Propadeutic, 7,10,60,64

Rational, 10–11,15,25,34,43–44,47,48,54–55,57,59,61,62,96–97,113–114,121
Religion, 1, 6

Religious relation, experience, 2,9,11, 46, 98—99,101—105,108,111—113,118—120, 122—124,127—128
Religiouness, 9,118—120,122—124,127—128
Romantics, 6, 8—9, 30—31
Savior, 3—4, 27, 49
Schelling, 14, 36
Self, 2—4,6—10,12—15,17,20,22—23,25,35,37,39—40,44,48—49,54—55,57,63,83,87,91—92,95—96,101,105,108—111,116—117,119,127
Socrates,2—4,21—24,27,29—31,34—39,48—49,55—58,60,82—84,100,114
Subjective, 2,3,9—12,20,22—23,25,28—29,37—38,44,46,52—55,87,89,91—95, 97—105,107—114,116,119,121—124,127—128
System, 1, 6, 10, 11, 19—20, 23, 77, 91, 99—100,106,107—111,126
Teacher, 2—4,20,23,25—34,36,48,56,59,82,84,130
The god, 4,7,11,23,25—27,31—35,39—44,46—51,56—63,73,76—89,92,95—97,101,105—111,113,119,121—123
Understanding, 4,26,31,33,35,39,40,43—48,52—58, 60—64,83,85—86, 101, 103,111,113—114,121—123
Vigilius Haufnensis, 28,130

www.ingramcontent.com/pod-product-compliance
Lightning Source LLC
Chambersburg PA
CBHW030116010526
44116CB00005B/268